CW00970333

COST OF CAPITAL:
THE APPLICATION OF FINANCIAL MODELS TO STATE AID

IAN ALEXANDER

THE OXERA PRESS

The OXERA Press is the imprint of Oxford Economic Research Associates Ltd.

Oxford Economic Research Associates Ltd
Blue Boar Court
Alfred Street
Oxford OX1 4EH
UK

ISBN 1 873482 24 8

CONTENTS

TABLES

FIGURES

FOREWORD

One of the most contentious areas of the relationship between government and industry is that of the provision of state aid. Several recent examples of the provision of state aid—to Groupe Bull, to Air France and to IRI of Italy (in relation to the restructuring and privatisation of its steel business, especially Ilva Laminati Piani)—have demonstrated the range of reactions that can arise from the announcement of government support for nationalised or private companies.

The provision of state aid is now dependent on the agreement of the European Commission (EC). To provide a framework for its deliberations, the EC set out a methodology known as the market economy investor principle (MEIP). Interpreting this framework has proved far from straightforward, as several of the state-aid cases have shown. Given the importance of state aid throughout Europe, it is, however, an area which requires further investigation. The basic thrust of the MEIP is that aid will be automatically granted only in cases where private investors would have been willing to provide funds if the company had been able to gain access to the relevant market. State aid can then be interpreted as the difference between the cost that the market would have levied on a private company for the provision of an equivalent amount of funds and the cost charged by the government.

This book sets out an approach that can be employed to assess whether private funds would have been made available for a project—whether the funds are intended for new investment or for restructuring. If the discounted cash flows arising from the provision of funds are positive, when discounted at a company's cost of capital, the funds should be treated as investment by the government rather than aid. Only if the present value of the cash flows is negative should the funds be considered as aid.

Although this methodology appears straightforward, it raises one serious question: what is the correct cost of capital for the company under investigation? Again, what should be a straightforward question poses problems. Many of the companies that receive state aid are nationalised and so no market data exists on which to base the required calculations. Also, the traditional cost-of-capital methodology was developed in relation to the Anglo-Saxon approach to finance. Much of Continental Europe follows a different model and so possible influences on the cost of capital need to be assessed.

This book has developed from a project undertaken for the UK Civil Aviation Authority (CAA) on state aid. The airline industry has been a particularly prominent industry in terms of the receipt of state aid. However, there is nothing unique about the airline industry that makes the methodology proposed any less applicable to other industries. It could be applied to nationalised industries, such as Electricité de France and Gaz de France or to private companies in receipt of state funds. Applying the

MEIP to state-run companies that are in competition with private companies offers one way of determining whether the state-run companies are placed at an unfair advantage by their relationship with the government. Would Société Nationale des Chemins de Fer (SNCF), the French rail company, warrant a, Aaa bond rating if it were privately owned? If not, how much more would the company have to pay for its debt finance and what implications would that have for competing transport companies? This makes the approach set out in this book powerful and versatile.

I would like to thank the EC for permission to quote from unpublished reports. The views expressed in this book are mine and not those of the CAA.

IAN ALEXANDER
MAY 1995

GLOSSARY

ACT	advance corporation tax
APT	arbitrage pricing theory
BA	British Airways
BZW	Barclays de Zoete Wedd
CAA	Civil Aviation Authority
CAPM	capital asset pricing model
CBI	Confederation of British Industry
CCA	current cost accounting
CSO	Central Statistical Office
DGM	dividend growth model
EC	European Commission
EFFAS	European Federation of Financial Analysts Societies
ERP	equity risk premium
EU	European Union
GDP	gross domestic product
GPA	Guinness Peat Aviation
IRR	internal rates of return
LBS	London Business School
MCT	mainstream corporation tax
MEIP	market economy investor principle
MMC	Monopolies and Mergers Commission
NFC	National Freight Corporation
OECD	Organisation for Economic Cooperation and Development
OFGAS	Office of Gas Supply
OFWAT	Office of Water Services
PE	price–earnings
SNCF	Société Nationale des Chemins de Fer
USM	unlisted securities market
WACC	weighted average cost of capital
WSA	Water Services Association

OVERVIEW

Financing from state governments to either nationalised or strategic industries can be interpreted in a number of ways. Either the state is injecting equity funds or it is providing aid to support an uncompetitive company. Being able to choose between these two possibilities is very important, as action may be required in the latter case owing to the possibility of anti-competitive behaviour. The European Commission has established its market economy investor principle to determine how the funds should be assessed. This book develops the ideas further and examines how the preferred methodology should be implemented.

At the heart of the methodology is the cost of capital. This provides a bench-mark against which the returns arising from the injection of funds can be measured. To determine the cost of capital, four separate areas need to be investigated.

Determining the cost of debt ought to be straightforward. A premium over and above the risk-free rate should be found for each company. Traditionally, the premium is calculated as the difference in redemption yields of a company bond and a government comparator bond. That may be possible for the UK, Germany, France and The Netherlands but may not be so easy for the other member states. Some of them may have active domestic bond markets, otherwise a second-best evaluation of bank borrowing rates has to be undertaken.

When calculating the cost of equity finance, it is usual to apply the capital asset pricing model (CAPM). This requires information on the risk-free rate, the equity risk premium (ERP) and the market risk of the company. Here, there are two problems. First, the traditional approach to evaluating one of these components, the ERP, is under attack. Second, the amount of data available for a number of the smaller economies means that the figures that can be found may not be suitable.

How these two costs of funds are combined is also important. It requires either a measure of gearing, or an evaluation of the sources of funds on a flow-of-funds basis. Both these approaches answer different questions, although the flow-of-funds approach is deemed more significant because of the marginal financing nature of the question of state aid.

Finally, the effects of taxation need to be considered. As comparisons are required for different countries, a pre-corporate-tax cost of capital must be established. The Ruding Committee provides a strong basis on which the impact of taxation can be assessed.

One problem that should be borne in mind while applying the preferred methodology is that the majority of companies in receipt of state aid are state-owned and so market information is not available. This does not invalidate the methodology, but forces the use of proxy information. Clearly, this means that any cost-of-capital figure found should be treated as an estimate.

Having established a bench-mark methodology, there are two separate questions that need to be addressed. First, is it applicable to the industry under review? Second, are there problems with the overall methodology?

Airlines are unusual, in as much as they have proved to be low-profit, high-investment companies. This has meant that the companies have sought tax-efficient sources of finance outside the traditional areas, especially leasing. There are two possible solutions to this problem. The cost of debt in the country in which the leasing is occurring can be taken as the true cost of capital, once the specific tax implications have been accommodated. Alternatively, since the government is effectively offering to provide equity finance, then only the cost of equity matters. Applying a cost-of-capital bench-mark is still the correct way of addressing this question.

Finally, there are institutional differences between countries that mean that a simple, mechanistic application of the bench-mark methodology is not applicable. First, as the expectations and attitudes of the investor groups are different between countries, attention needs to be given to the influence that this can have. Also, lending practices may differ, either in terms of the criteria employed or the way in which financial distress is approached. This again may effectively raise or lower the cost of capital.

The bench-mark developed here is the first, important step to determining whether the government funds are state aid or new finance. Once this quantitative hurdle has been addressed, two situations can arise. If the return on the funds clears the hurdle, nothing else need happen. If it fails to clear the hurdle, more qualitative information is required so that these additional problems can be addressed. There is bound to be a grey area into which some of the financing requests fall. The aim of this book is, however, to ensure that the grey area is minimised.

1. INTRODUCTION

In its 1993 document, 'Airline Competition in the Single European Market', the Civil Aviation Authority (CAA) raised a number of concerns related to the use by the European Commission (EC) of the market economy investor principle (MEIP). This methodology is employed in the assessment of whether government subsidies to domestic companies are anti-competitive. Two cases were highlighted in the document: Air France and Groupe Bull. In the first case, the application of the MEIP led to a general discussion of the company and its future prospects, while in the second, a very detailed comparison of historic returns and future prospects was undertaken. In an area as important as that of state aid, this sort of diversity of approach provides no stable framework for assessing individual cases and so creates uncertainty. This is likely to prove detrimental for both companies and governments.

This book considers how a set of formal guidelines for the application of the MEIP can be established. Having a clear, comprehensive and practical methodology for the assessment of government subsidies would remove the ambiguity of the current guidelines and ensure that all cases are treated equally. It would also ensure that companies and governments knew what information has to be provided to the Commission when an MEIP study was being undertaken.

Under the MEIP, the obvious bench-mark against which any proposed subsidy or fresh injection of public funds should be evaluated is the cost at which the financial markets would be willing to provide funds. This is the cost of capital for a company. If the proposed subsidy leads to returns greater than the cost of capital, an injection of funds by a government can be treated as new finance rather than state aid. If the returns are below the cost of capital, the subsidy is clearly state aid and therefore needs to be considered in terms of competition policy.

The structure of the book is as follows. Chapter 2 establishes the framework for the analysis. This is followed by two chapters which describe the traditional approach to calculating the cost of capital. Each of the principal sources of finance, the cost of debt and the cost of equity, are discussed. These provide a clear framework within which the cost of capital can be estimated for a company. Alternative approaches are assessed, with a consideration of tax questions and the proportions of each type of finance employed. However, there are reasons to believe that there are problems with applying this approach internationally and each chapter also, therefore, evaluates critically how these principles have been applied in practice. There are a number of academic and public-body studies that have attempted to evaluate either the cost of capital, or constituent parts of the cost of capital, on an international basis. The approaches that have been adopted are compared to our theoretical bench-mark and any reasons for deviation are assessed.

Problems with the methodology developed here may not be confined to purely practical problems highlighted by earlier attempts to apply the approach. There are a number of institutional factors that also have a bearing on the question. These are investigated in chapters 8 and 9. If there are institutional differences between countries, further questions about how the MEIP should be applied may be raised. The differences may arise in the form of financial institutions that exist, or the approaches to evaluating investments that they apply. Each of these possible problem areas is considered and the evidence reviewed. Effectively, these chapters examine whether the perceived differences between the Anglo-Saxon model of finance—employed in the UK and Ireland—and the Continental European model—as exemplified by Germany and France—are as important as some commentators suggest.

Even if significant institutional differences are found, this does not invalidate the use of the cost of capital as a bench-mark for the MEIP. What they imply is that this approach may be difficult to apply when undertaking international comparisons. The overall purpose of the book is to provide the best-practice approach to establishing a bench-mark for assessing whether government funds should be considered as state aid or equity finance. A clear, practical set of guidelines for applying the MEIP will benefit all parties involved.

2. FRAMEWORK OF THE ANALYSIS

Evaluating the implications of state financing for industry raises a number of important questions. In the introduction it was stated that the cost of capital provides an efficient bench-mark against which aid should be assessed. Why is this so? Even if the cost of capital is the correct bench-mark, is it possible to undertake comparisons of the cost of capital between countries? Finally, if it is possible to undertake such comparisons, are they relevant to the airline industry? These questions are addressed in this chapter.

Relevance of the cost of capital

Why should a government provide funds to a company? Either the funds are an injection of capital on which the government expects the company to earn a suitable rate of return, or the government is providing aid to support an uncompetitive operation. Making a distinction between these two very different situations depends on being able to assess the impact of the state financing on the returns of the company, or on a specific project.

Important in this decision-making process is the determination of the cut-off point above which returns are deemed economic and below which any funds should be counted as aid. For a private company, this cut-off point is its cost of capital. If the financial markets are unwilling to lend funds at such a rate as to make a new project profitable, the project would not be undertaken. The cost of those funds is determined by the risk of the project.

There is no reason to judge public companies differently. The state's funds ought to be treated as equity finance, no interest is required but a 'dividend' should be paid at some point. The cost of capital appears to be the relevant bench-mark against which state funds should be assessed.

Choice of market

Before examining the elements of the cost of capital, it is worth establishing which markets should be considered. Capital markets are now international, funds flow from country to country at the whim of speculators and investors. Should the international markets be the focus of our attention or the domestic markets? If the international markets for debt and equity provide the bulk of the funds for industry, the common elements of the bench-mark calculation should be determined at this level. However, if the domestic markets are the main source, those common elements will be determined at a national level for each member country.

Although capital markets are truly international, few companies can be considered as such. The top few hundred companies in the world have access to most financial markets but the majority of companies have access to only one or two. There are two principal reasons for this. First, the profile required for access to the international markets is denied to most companies. Either the companies are not geographically represented in certain areas, or the cost of maintaining one brand name is prohibitive, given the size of the company. Second, certain markets are effectively closed to all but domestic companies. This artificial barrier may be due to government policy or it may simply be that the size of the market does not make it attractive to international companies. Several of the smaller European countries, such as Greece and Portugal, have equity and debt markets that attract few foreign companies. Because of these considerations, it would appear that concentrating on domestic markets is the correct approach to this question.

That assessment may be correct for the equity markets but, for debt, a more international approach may be required. The growth of the Euro-markets has created a truly international debt market. Concentrating on domestic debt markets could provide very misleading results in this type of study. Until recently, only the government had access to the UK debt market; companies raised Euro-based fixed-interest securities in preference to domestic ones. It would appear, therefore, that some consideration of this Euro-market is also warranted.

Determination of the cost of capital

Before considering the components of the cost of capital, it is worth establishing the relevant measure. Although state-owned companies dominate the airline industry in Europe, the correct measure that should be employed is that of a private company. The reason for this is that considering the state's cost of capital would, in itself, imply a subsidy for the airline. As the question of state aid is concerned with how a company is being advantaged relative to other companies, the relevant bench-mark must be the cost of capital for a private company.

When establishing the cost of capital, the standard approach is to calculate a weighted average cost of capital (WACC), which consists of four elements:

- the cost of debt finance;
- the cost of equity finance;
- the proportions of each type of finance employed (gearing);
- taxation.

Each of these is considered in detail in chapters of this book. For each approach the standard methodology employed in establishing the value is explained and then critically assessed. In those areas where debate exists on specific points the nature of the debate and the possible implications for the cost of capital are considered.

Numerous studies have already been undertaken to attempt to determine the cost of capital in different countries. An example of the type of results found by these studies is provided in Figure 1, which uses data collected by the Federal Reserve Bank of New York. Where possible the approaches adopted in these studies are also critically assessed in the relevant chapters of the book.

Figure 1: Annual cost of capital for equipment and machinery (1977–88)

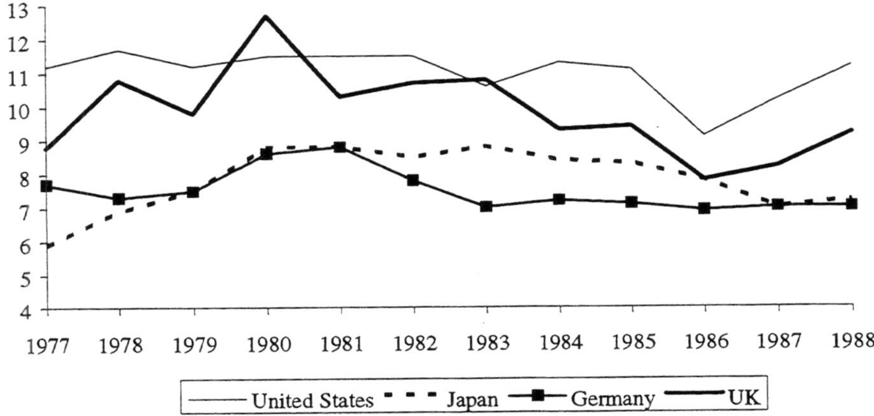

Source: Federal Reserve Bank of New York.

Institutional differences

One important lesson from previous studies is that the mechanistic application of simple formulae may provide misleading or incorrect information. Consideration of values derived from the cost-of-capital equations without placing them in the context of the country's institutional framework can lead to conclusions that fail to address the important issues. Germany may appear to have a high cost of capital, but if the financial markets take a very lenient attitude towards supporting industry through periods of crisis, the implications of the high cost of capital should be reassessed.

Considerations of the financial structures in the various member countries and the possible impact that they can have on this bench-mark analysis is provided in the later chapters of this book. These problems should not be seen as a bar to using this bench-marking approach but as caveats applying to whatever results are found.

Relevance to the airline industry

Establishing a cost-of-capital methodology that is applicable to a country-by-country study is only relevant to this decision if it can be applied to the industry in receipt of state aid. Airlines, along with steel and rail, are the most heavily 'subsidised' industries in the European Union (EU). It would be pointless developing a methodology that was not applicable to those industries where it is required.

There are a number of features specific to the airline industry. Tables 2.1 and 2.2 provide information on the ownership and profitability of the airline companies in the member countries.

Table 2.1: Ownership of national flag carriers (1993)

Airline	Country	% owned by state		Publicly listed	Foreign state-controlled companies
		Direct	Indirect		
Aer Lingus	Ireland	100.0	0.0	0.0	0.0
Air France	France	98.6	0.0	1.4	0.0
Alitalia	Italy	86.4	0.0	13.6	0.0
BA	UK	0.0	0.0	100.0	0.0
Iberia	Spain	0.0	99.8	0.2	0.0
KLM	Netherlands	38.2	0.0	61.8	0.0
Lufthansa	Germany	51.4	5.5	43.1	0.0
Luxair	Luxemburg	23.1	26.3	37.6	13.0
Olympic	Greece	100.0	0.0	0.0	0.0
Sabena	Belgium	61.8	0.0	0.7	37.5
SAS	Denmark	0.0	28.6	0.0	71.4
TAP	Portugal	100.0	0.0	0.0	0.0

Source: CAA.

Table 2.2: Financial performance of Community airlines

	Group sales ($m)	Operating profit ($m)	Net profit ($m)	Net margin (%)
Aer Lingus	1,381	–78	–196	–14.2
Air France	10,769	–285	–617	–5.7
Alitalia	5,511	209	–12	–0.2
BA	9,308	518	298	3.2
Iberia	4,137	–120	–340	–8.2
Lufthansa	11,037	–199	–250	–2.3
Luxair	253	n/a	1	0.2
Olympus	923	–35	–255	–24.4
Sabena	1,708	61	12	0.7
SAS	5,908	503	–127	–2.2
TAP	1,110	–74	–200	–18.0
Total	52,045	500	–1,686	–3.2

Note: The data is for the financial year ending March 1993 for BA and Aer Lingus and December 1992 for the other groups. Net margin is the proportion the net profit forms of group sales.
Source: *Airline Business*, September 1993 and reproduced by the CAA.

Tables 2.1 and 2.2 show that the majority of national flag carriers are still primarily state-owned. Only British Airways (BA) and KLM have more than 50% of their equity in private hands, with private investors holding significant minority stakes in Lufthansa and Luxair. This suggests that the question of state aid is an important one for the airline industry.

Table 2.2 illustrates quite clearly one of the problems facing airlines: the majority of them are not profitable once financing costs have been paid. Airlines are notorious for being loss-making, hence the number that are nationalised. This has an important effect on the type of financing that these companies choose to employ. Traditionally, the cost-of-capital question has concentrated on the cost of debt and the cost of equity. Airlines employ leasing finance because it is tax-efficient for low-profitability companies facing high-investment projects. This does not invalidate a consideration of the traditional sources of finance. It means, however, that, when employing the preferred methodology to establish a bench-mark, the correct cost of debt—the heart of the leasing decision—is identified.

Non-listed companies

One important problem that should be borne in mind when considering the airline industry in Europe is that of non-listed companies. The majority of airlines, especially flag-carriers, are either owned by the state or are private companies, as Table 2.1 showed. This raises a serious data problem when considering the cost of capital. Much of the information that is required for any methodology is based on observed market data. For the non-listed companies this is not available.

There are four listed airlines in the EU. These are shown in Table 2.3, along with a number of other airline companies that could be used to provide comparative information.

Table 2.3: Quoted airline companies

Country	Company
EU	
Germany	Lufthansa
Italy	Alitalia
Netherlands	KLM
UK	British Airways
Other	
Japan	All Nippon Airlines
Japan	JAL
Hong Kong	Cathay Pacific
Switzerland	Swiss Air
America	Delta
America	UAL

A selection of the other quoted airlines has been given; obviously there are many more American companies.

The fact that there are other airlines that can be used for comparison does not necessarily make the situation any easier with regard to the non-listed airlines. It is important that the business spread, geographical spread and degree of competition faced is investigated before any comparison is made. The way in which these various factors influence the cost-of-capital calculation will be discussed in later chapters.

Additional complications

A number of general points need to be made before we move on to the more detailed investigation. These fall into two categories: the ability to compare international figures and the availability of data.

International comparisons

When making international comparisons there are several important additional considerations.

- *Real rates of return*. A comparison of the actual cost of capital is influenced by the inflation rate, as nominal interest rates and costs of equity will be employed. The observed nominal cost of capital will be different across countries owing to the different rates of inflation. There are also different expectations of future inflation between countries. Concentrating on the real, inflation-adjusted, cost of capital provides one way of overcoming this problem.

- *Exchange rate*. Where actual levels and amounts are considered, normally as supporting evidence, an average annual exchange rate should be applied to convert everything into a common currency.

Data availability

Data availability is important for two reasons. First, access to primary sources of data is limited for a number of the smaller countries. This may be a general problem and certain of the principles developed in this book may not be entirely applicable to every country. An example of this is the expected inflation rate for Greece. In such cases, second-best estimates or information will have to be applied.

Second, a distinction needs to be drawn between *ex ante* and *ex post* data. The first of these, *ex ante*, is concerned with what is expected to happen, while the second, *ex post*, is a reflection of what actually happened. Although *ex post* data is available for many of the items required, it is clear in chapter 4 that *ex ante* data is most useful. However, this is also the data that is hardest to quantify, let alone find from secondary sources.

International studies

An important concern of this book is the available evidence on the cost of capital in different European countries. There are three main studies of the cost of capital that will be referred to throughout and one comprehensive study of the tax implications. These studies are:

- Federal Reserve Bank of New York, 'Explaining International Differences in the Cost of Capital'. This was published in 1989 and considers four countries, two of which, Germany and the UK, are of interest to this study.

- Coopers & Lybrand, 'Final Report for the Study on International Differences in the Cost of Capital for European Commission.' This report for the EC studies the cost of capital in each of the member countries, using data from 1991. The results are set out in Appendix 1.

- EC, 'The Cost of Capital'. This paper draws together a number of tables from different EC sources and uses them to highlight some of the theory that the paper discusses. The date for this is uncertain, although it would appear to be either 1991 or 1992.

- EC, 'Report of the Committee of Independent Experts on Company Taxation', 1992. This was the final report of the Ruding Committee, so-called after its chairman, Onno Ruding, and is referred to as such throughout the book.

3. DIFFERENCES IN DEBT COSTS OF CAPITAL

The cost of debt finance plays two roles in the cost-of-capital calculation. First, the risk-free rate is a measure of the cost of debt for the government of a country. This is important in estimating both the cost of equity finance and the cost of debt, since it provides the bench-mark against which investors measure all risky returns. Second, the rate at which companies can raise debt finance is relevant. This cost is normally quoted as a premium over the government risk-free rate.

Measurement of the cost of debt

Before considering the two roles that the cost of debt plays, it is important to clarify exactly how the cost of debt is determined. The standard approach is to consider the redemption yield—also referred to as the yield to maturity—on a government fixed-interest security. A redemption yield is calculated as:

$$P_0 = \sum_{t=0}^{t=n} \frac{C_t}{(1+\rho)^t} + \frac{R}{(1+\rho)^n}$$

Where: ρ is the redemption yield;
P is the current market price of the security;
C is the coupon paid in each period;
R is the redeemable face value of the security;
n is the number of periods until the redemption of the security.

The redemption yield is normally quoted as an annualised rate and can be interpreted as an interest rate.

Variations in government risk-free rates

As chapter 2 highlighted, it is important to consider real interest rates across countries rather than actual interest rates. Table 3.1 contains information on real interest rates from the member countries.

The fact that some of these estimates are negative raises an important point. The figures are out-turn estimates of the true expected real interest rate. This *ex post/ex ante* split is very important and is discussed in detail in chapter 4.

Table 3.1: Real interest rates

Country	Real interest rate		
	1980	**1985**	**1991**
Belgium	6.0	4.6	6.4
Denmark	8.2	6.9	7.2
France	0.5	7.1	7.0
Germany	2.7	4.9	5.8
Greece	–4.0	–2.5	–1.2
Ireland	–3.3	7.7	6.3
Italy	–4.1	4.3	6.4
Luxemburg	–0.1	3.5	5.0
Netherlands	3.1	5.0	6.5
Portugal	–4.7	5.8	3.9
Spain	–0.1	5.2	8.4
UK	–2.5	5.2	4.2

Source: Ruding Committee (1992); Eurostat.

No clear attempt has been made to establish the *ex ante* estimate of real interest rates in the member countries. Only in the UK, where index-linked gilts have been issued, is it possible to establish a good estimate of this figure. Even that estimate has some drawbacks owing to the inability to remove inflation risk completely. A recent paper by Blanchard (1993), discussed in chapter 4, provides an attempt at deriving real *ex ante* risk-free rates for several countries. The figures are provided in Appendix 2.

Although the methodology is clear, the estimation of a real risk-free rate requires the use of nominal government bond yields and an expected inflation rate for all countries except the UK. This poses a few problems.

It is unclear whether the Ruding Committee data is based on redemption yields or other measures of interest rates. To show the effect of using redemption yields, data was collected for those companies where it is readily available. The results are shown in Table 3.2.

The redemption yields employed are based on bond indices calculated by Datastream and the European Federation of Financial Analysts Societies (EFFAS). They consist of 'representative' government issues (for instance, no zero coupon or perpetuals) selected by EFFAS members. The expected inflation figures are taken from *Consensus Forecasts* and are a simple average of the estimate for 1994 and 1995. One obvious problem with this approach is that the maturity of the bonds will be substantially above two years, thereby making the above estimates prone to errors. The UK figure is substantially above that derived from using index-linked bonds, although recent inflation expectations shown in the Bank of England Inflation Report (May) show a peak above 6% within the next few years. Table 3.2 serves, however, as an example of the sort of approach that should be undertaken.

Table 3.2: Risk-free rates based on redemption yields

Country	Redemption yield June 1st 1994	Inflation estimate May 9th 1994	Real risk-free rate
Belgium	7.8	2.6	5.2
Denmark	7.9	2.3	5.6
France	7.5	1.9	5.6
Germany	6.8	2.6	4.2
Ireland	8.7	2.8	5.9
Italy	10.3	3.7	6.6
Netherlands	7.1	2.5	4.6
Spain	9.5	4.1	5.4
UK	9.0	3.2	5.8

Source: Datastream and *Consensus Forecasts* (May 1994); author's own calculations.

Differences in debt margins across countries

Having established a base risk-free rate, it is necessary to ascertain the premium above this that a company has to pay. Again, in principle, this process ought to be straightforward. If the company under consideration has issued tradable bonds, it is possible to derive a redemption yield using the formula given earlier. A comparator bond—a government bond issue of similar maturity and coupon—is chosen and the difference in redemption yields is the debt premium.

Although traded Euro-market bonds often only account for a small proportion of a company's total debt, it is assumed that all this debt carries the same premium. The rationale behind this is linked to the fact that the Euro-markets ought to be providing the cheapest source of debt finance and so Eurobonds provide a good estimate of the marginal cost of debt.

However, the majority of airlines do not have access to the Euro-markets and this simple approach cannot be used. Two alternative methodologies can be employed to overcome this problem:

- establish an implied credit rating for the company and determine what level of debt premium this provides;

- consider those debt markets in which the companies operate and calculate a debt premium on a different financial instrument.

These methodologies are considered in the following sub-sections.

Establishing a credit rating

Most analysis of establishing a credit rating has been performed on US companies, although some research on non-US companies has been undertaken—more often in relation to the risk of bankruptcy through Z scores rather than establishing an implied credit rating. Multi-country credit ratings are produced by two US companies, Moody's and Standard & Poor's, and one UK company, IBCA, although the last concentrates on financial institutions. To provide an example of the level of information available on European companies, Table 3.3 summarises Moody's credit ratings in May 1994.

Table 3.3: European company ratings

Country	No. of rated companies	Companies with short-term ratings only	No. with Aaa ratings	No. with ratings of A3 or above
Belgium	9	1	0	8
Denmark	17	2	0	15
France	58	8	18	46
Germany	33	3	12	28
Greece	2	0	0	0
Ireland	5	0	0	3
Italy	20	3	0	15
Luxemburg	0	0	0	0
Netherlands	15	3	5	11
Portugal	2	0	0	2
Spain	23	2	0	21
UK	126	32	6	81

Source: Moody's 'Global Ratings Guide', May 1994.

Table 3.3 highlights a number of important facts. First, apart from the largest companies, few have access to the Euro-markets. Second, those which do have access to these markets appear to be concentrated at the higher end of the rating spectrum for the majority of European countries. Table 3.3 does not, however, show the importance of financial institutions in terms of ratings. The majority of Aaa-rated companies are financial institutions, rather than industrial and commercial companies. This explains why the UK has such a large number of lower-rated companies, since it is much more common for UK industrial and commercial companies to have access to the international debt markets.

A further point that should be stressed is that only one member country airline has a credit rating from Moody's. BA is rated A2. In some respects, therefore, this avenue of investigation is only of limited worth. For the majority of countries, it should be possible to establish a relationship between a level of rating and a debt premium, but ensuring that this is the correct relationship for an airline could only be verified in one country.

Closer investigation of the French credit ratings provides an interesting area of consideration for the question of state aid. Five of the 18 Aaa-rated companies are state-controlled industrial and commercial enterprises, including SNCF, Electricité de France and France Télécom. Whether these companies would have an Aaa rating if they were not state-controlled is an important consideration. If the companies can raise debt finance at a cheaper rate than other similar companies, should this be considered aid? The highest rating is achieved through an implicit government guarantee; if that guarantee did not exist, the rating could be lower.

Estimating the debt premium

From the available companies, it is possible either to estimate a credit rating or to estimate the debt premium directly. As there is an element of qualitative information contained in any credit-rating decision, a more profitable route is to try to observe the debt premium directly.

It is fairly well documented that certain specific financial ratios have an impact on the observed debt premium. The most relevant of these are:

- interest cover;
- gearing;
- size of company;
- size of debt issue;
- maturity of debt issue;
- a measure of cash flow or profits.

Using regressions it should be possible to derive relationships between the observed debt premium and the observed financial information. This relationship could then be used to estimate a debt premium for an airline using the available financial information.

Two cautionary points need to be considered. First, sufficient observations are required to ensure that the relationship found is suitable for general application to other companies. This requires both a large number of separate companies and a long time-series of data for each company. These two data requirements ensure that the impact of the changing economic climate is adequately accommodated and that a wide enough spread of companies is considered. It is obvious that these conditions could not be met for all countries.

Second, as discussed in chapter 2, airlines are unusual in the very high level of leasing finance that is employed. This would be outside the scope of the majority of financial indicators employed in the estimation process. Whether the level of interest cover would indicate adequately the impact of leasing could vary from country to country according to accounting conventions.

There is, therefore, a process for estimating directly the debt premium a company should pay over its government's risk-free rate. Whether this process can be applied to the smaller countries is debatable. It is also unclear whether the unusual attributes of the airline industry will invalidate any general relationship found from an investigation of other industrial and commercial companies.

Other debt markets

The second alternative to observing directly the cost of debt on Euro-market fixed-interest securities is to consider debt premia in other markets. There are a number of such markets, which are discussed below.

Domestic bond markets

Even if a company is not active in the international bond markets, this does not mean that it does not raise fixed-interest security finance. There may be an active domestic bond market. If one exists, it should be possible to observe directly a debt premium over and above the government's borrowing rate for an equivalent security. This can be treated in the same way as any other debt premium.

If there is an active domestic market but no debt issued by the airline, it could be possible to estimate a relationship based on the approach outlined above, where domestic bond premia are substituted for Euro-bond premia. Before undertaking such a process, two important questions need to be addressed. First, how deep is the market? Liquidity problems in any section of the domestic market could lead to observed premia being influenced by forces other than the financial indicators of the company. Second, the tax treatment of the government and corporate bonds needs to be assessed. If there are differences in tax treatment, the observed premia will be partly a reflection of the tax-clientele effect.

Bank debt

Information on the premium companies pay over bank base rates is often available in some form for each country. Some countries, France, Germany and the UK, provide quite detailed information on corporate borrowing rates, while for others less information is easily available. The relevant margin over the bank base rate could be used as a proxy for the true cost of debt, although the observable rates for any individual company will be both historical and an average rather than a marginal financing figure.

Valuing guarantees

One of the important forms of government aid available to companies, both state-owned and private, is guaranteed debt finance. Rather than actually provide funds directly from the Treasury, or Ministry of Finance, the state provides a guarantee for the company, permitting it to raise external funds on its own account. This guarantee could take many forms, the most common is that of guaranteeing the interest payments and the redemption on fixed-interest securities.

As was seen in Table 3.3 and its associated paragraphs, French state-owned companies make an important use of this type of provision which allows them then to borrow at the same credit rating as the government, Aaa. Although the rating is the same as the government's, it is likely that some premium will exist as the company's debt may not be perfectly guaranteed. There may be questions about the speed with which the government would step in to support a company or even whether it would honour its guarantees. Often these sorts of question are related to private companies that have implicit state guarantees, such as Eurotunnel.

What is the value of this type of guarantee? If a company is able to borrow at a smaller debt premium than would have been the case had it raised the finance for itself, then the impact of the guarantee is the amount by which the premium was lowered. When assessing the bench-mark cost of debt finance it is the 'true' cost that should be considered rather than the guaranteed cost. Two related approaches exist for determining the impact of applying guarantees.

First, if sufficient companies exist that have guarantees, then when modelling the debt premium it is possible to introduce a dummy variable for the existence of guarantees. The approach to estimating debt premia set out earlier would simply need to have this term added. Then, once the coefficient on the dummy variable has been estimated, it would be possible to estimate the basis-point impact of having a guarantee. This figure could then be added back on to the known debt premium to provide the 'true' figure.

An alternative, and preferable, approach depends on the use of known financial ratios to establish the debt premium from scratch, rather than applying an adjustment to the observed figure. This is preferable as the first approach assumes a common impact of a guarantee, while the actual effect ought to be based on the credit-rating class that a company would belong to if its rating were not obscured by the guarantee.

Whether sufficient data is available to carry out this sort of analysis for each of the countries is debatable. It ought to be possible to study it for a number of the countries, however, especially France where this type of government support is prevalent.

Evidence from international studies

The international studies, discussed in chapter 2, employed various approaches to establishing the cost of debt.

The Federal Reserve Bank of New York

This study considers the cost of debt as the real post-tax rate of interest faced by non-financial companies. Adjustments are made according to national proportions of type of debt instrument, the borrowing costs of different liquidities of asset, inflation and taxation. Although the bond finance is treated as detailed above—a redemption yield on a specific type of bond is employed—the bank finance rates appear to be less easy to find. No clear evidence is provided in the study as to how a figure was derived for this part of the cost of debt.

The inflation adjustment is based on individual country gross domestic product (GDP) deflators, the best estimate of inflation, although no attempt is made to use expected inflation figures and the UK and West Germany therefore had negative real costs of debt finance in the late 1970s.

Coopers & Lybrand

Appendix 1 contains the results table of the Coopers & Lybrand study. For the risk-free rate, the redemption yield—yield to maturity—for long-dated government bonds is employed. This provides a nominal rate from which a medium-term estimate of inflation is subtracted, covering the period of 5–10 years, obtained from *Consensus*

Forecasts. There is no attempt to verify the figure derived for the UK against the appropriate index-linked security, which would have helped validate the process.

To find the cost of debt, two additional pieces of information are used. First, historic averages of the premium on corporate bonds and bank lending rates over short-term money-market rates are calculated. An average, based on the relative proportions of each of these types of debt, is then calculated and added to the risk-free rate. This process may be flawed for three reasons.

First, it is assumed that the same mix of debt instruments will be used in the financing of a new project. The capital structure of companies is, in some senses, a historical event, the marginal financing structure is of much more interest. Second, should averages have been used? As this project was seeking a snapshot of the cost of capital, a spot estimate would have been more reliable. Finally, the premia should have been measured against the same instrument that was employed in the risk-free rate, rather than a separate money-market rate.

European Commission study

The EC study does not approach the cost of debt in such a traditional way. Although risk-free rates are evaluated through a consideration of long-term interest rates, it is uncertain how inflation is accounted for. The paper accepts that inflation expectations are important but does not go on to explain how it derives its figures when calculating a real figure. Given the time-span investigated, it is likely that the figures used are historical out-turn figures, rather than expectations.

When the study considers the debt premia paid by companies there is more convincing evidence, although, as with the estimates in Coopers & Lybrand study, average financial structures rather than marginal ones are considered. Evidence is provided on the prevalence of Euro-Commercial Paper, the split between short- and medium- to long-term debt employed in companies' balance sheets—a notoriously difficult piece of information to construct on a truly comparable basis owing to the differences in accounting practice throughout the member states—and the spread paid for various types of debt. Those spreads are reproduced in Table 3.4. They suffer from similar problems to those encountered in the Coopers & Lybrand study, in that the instrument against which they are measured is inconsistent with the risk-free rate.

Implications for the bench-mark

Two points have been addressed in this chapter, the risk-free rate and the debt premium that a company pays for debt finance. There is very little controversy over the way these should be calculated. The redemption yield on an index-linked bond is the best-possible estimate of the risk-free rate. For debt premia, the difference between the redemption yield of a corporate bond and a comparable government bond is the preferred approach.

In relation to the risk-free rate, only one country in Europe has issued index-linked bonds, the UK. A second-best approach is to take the redemption yield on a nominal bond and subtract the expected level of inflation over the lifetime of the bond. This

Table 3.4: Bank spread estimations (end 1990), %

	Spread 1	Spread 2	Spread 3
High Spread			
Portugal	7.59	n/a	n/a
France	6.92	3.14	6.46
Belgium	4.88	1.14	3.06
Germany	3.67	n/a	2.66
Netherlands	3.29	n/a	2.49
Low Spread			
Denmark	1.98	2.70	3.40
Spain	1.20	2.40	0.82
Italy	1.08	1.15	1.29
Ireland	–0.10	n/a	–0.08
UK	–0.26	1.69	0.69

Note: Spread 1 refers to the lending rate minus the money-market rate. Spread 2 refers to the rate charged to borrowers for short- to medium-term loans minus the typical short-term rate. Spread 3 is the lending rate minus the typical short-term rate.

provides an *ex ante* estimate of the risk-free rate. For the majority of member countries this approach is possible; Blanchard calculated it using estimates of inflation made by DRI, a financial consultancy. This may not be possible for a number of the smaller member countries, however, owing to the lack of an estimate of future inflation. *Consensus Forecasts* provides ten-year forecasts of inflation for France, Germany, Italy and the UK, but only two-year forecasts for the other EC member countries. For those countries with short-term, or no, forecasts, an *ex post* estimate will be the best available. Many more problems exist for the estimation of corporate debt premia.

Only the four largest European economies have many companies gaining access to the Euro-debt markets, and only one airline has tapped this source of funds. Relying on domestic bond markets offers an acceptable solution to the problem, provided that they are sufficiently liquid. Being forced to use bank-lending margins is a poor substitute, but it may have to be used in some cases.

Overall, the problems raised by the cost of debt tend to be those related to data availability rather than fundamental theoretical differences of opinion. These problems are not insoluble and an estimate will always be available for the cost of debt. It may be, however, that, for some of the smaller member countries, the estimate has to be accepted with quite a large margin of error.

4. ESTIMATING THE COST OF EQUITY

Although the majority of member-country airlines are state-owned (see Table 2.1), the cost of equity finance is still an important concept. Any state funds invested in the company ought to be treated as equity finance, unless there is a clear interest-rate and repayment structure applied to the finance. Also, if a company were raising external finance, equity would be an important element of any financing package. Chapter 7 discusses the actual proportions of the different forms of finance used in each country.

Estimating the cost of equity finance can be done by using one of three models:

- the arbitrage pricing theory (APT);
- the dividend growth model (DGM);
- the capital asset pricing model (CAPM).

The third of these, the CAPM, is the standard methodology employed by most companies, regulators and governments. Although the other models may have individual characteristics that are preferable to those of the CAPM, no other model has yet proved capable of displacing it. This is not to say that the CAPM is a good predictor of the true cost of capital, simply that it is better than the alternatives. This chapter concentrates on the CAPM, while chapter 5 considers some quite different approaches to the whole question of the cost of equity and the cost of debt.

The capital asset pricing model

Although this model is based on stylised assumptions concerning the efficiency of capital markets and the effects of the level of friction that exists, no other theory has provided a better estimate of the cost of equity. The CAPM is effectively a simple relationship between the level of return for an individual company and a number of market-wide variables. The equation underlying the CAPM is given below:

$$E(r_i)=r_f+\beta_i[E(r_m)-r_f]$$

Here $E(r)$ is the expected level of return, i indicates an individual company and m stands for the whole market. b (beta) is a measure of the undiversifiable risk of a company and is defined as:

$$\beta_i=\frac{\text{covariance}(r_i r_m)}{\text{variance}(r_m)}$$

The final term in the CAPM equation is the risk-free rate, r_f, which was discussed in length in chapter 3.

Establishing the cost of equity finance requires the calculation of each of these values for the company or country under consideration. Two problems can arise when this sort of estimation is undertaken. First, although the overall form of the CAPM equation is accepted, there is still debate about certain parts of it. This is especially true of the equity risk premium (ERP)—the difference between the level of expected return on the market and the risk-free rate. Second, research into the constituent parts of the CAPM has concentrated on the UK, US and Japan. This means that there is little comparative data available for the other European countries.

Two elements of the equation will be discussed in this chapter; the ERP and the beta value.

Equity risk premia

The ERP is the most debated part of the cost of equity. It is a measure of the additional return an investor requires in order to hold a portfolio covering the complete equity market rather than the risk-free asset. The definition of the ERP is:

$$ERP = E(r_m) - E(r_f)$$

It is made up of two elements: the expected level of return on the market and the risk-free rate. In principle, both ought to be easy to calculate but, in practice, there are several problems. This section is structured as follows. First, the traditional approach to estimating the ERP is outlined. The standard problems associated with this are then investigated. Finally, the newer methodologies are investigated.

The traditional approach

When estimating the ERP, two sets of time-series information are traditionally employed. Out-turn levels of market return and government bond redemption yields are collected for as long a period as possible, with the difference between the series being the ERP. An arithmetic average of this time-series of ERP figures is employed to estimate the expected level to be included in the CAPM formula.

For the UK the dataset normally employed in this estimation process is that provided by Barclays de Zoete Wedd (BZW). An annual publication, 'The Equity Gilt Study', gives information on returns from 1919 to the present date. If information from the 1994 edition is employed in the estimation process, the following figures are found.

Table 4.1: The traditional equity risk premium

Average annual return (%)	1919–93	1946–93	1963–93
Equity	10.19	9.18	9.57
Gilt	3.00	0.78	2.69
ERP	7.19	8.40	6.87

Source: Jenkinson, 1994.

As can be seen, the figures are very sensitive to the period chosen. This style of calculation can easily be undertaken for each of the markets and an ERP estimated for each country.

Averaging processes

The first area of debate raised by this traditional approach concerns the averaging process employed. There are two contenders, arithmetic and geometric averages. An assumption underlying the CAPM is that equity markets are efficient. One interpretation of this is that returns to shareholders are random. When averaging a random series, the arithmetic average is the correct one to use. If returns were not random, it would be possible for investors to predict the way in which share prices will move and so continually 'beat the market' in terms of investment policy. This would invalidate the principle of efficient markets.

However, there is some evidence of short-term mean reversion in share prices that may lead to the arithmetic average producing a biased result. If this is the case, there may be reason to believe that the geometric average provides a better estimate of the true ERP. To illustrate the importance of this question, consider Table 4.2 where the figures from Jenkinson (1994) are reproduced with both types of average.

Table 4.2: The effect of the choice of averaging process

	1919–93	1946–93	1963–93
Arithmetic returns (%)			
Equity	10.19	9.18	9.57
Gilt	3.00	0.78	2.69
ERP	7.19	8.40	6.87
Geometric returns (%)			
Equity	7.84	6.65	6.42
Gilt	2.09	0.05	1.93
ERP	5.76	6.60	4.49

Source: Jenkinson, 1994.

The process chosen appears to have an important effect, although the choice may not be so stark. Research undertaken by Blume (1974) proposed that the true unbiased estimate of a set of returns is:

$$E(R_N)=\left[\left(\frac{T-N}{T-1}\right)\times A^N\right]+\left[\left(\frac{N-1}{T-1}\right)\times G^N\right]$$

$$E(R_N)=M^N$$

where A is the arithmetic mean of the sample of T data points and G is the geometric mean. N is the number of periods over which the estimate is being made. M is the unbiased estimate of the true average. As the number of periods involved in the estimation increases, ie as N grows larger, the weight attached to A falls. The period 1919–93, the longest time-run available for the estimation of an ERP, provides 74 data points. If a five-year investment period is assumed, then 95% of the weight is attached to A. If a 40-year investment period is assumed, the weight falls to 45%.

Computational problems

There may be two problems with the available dataset. First, how representative is the ERP? Second, does the composition of the dataset change over time?

In relation to the first of these questions consider Table 4.3, which provides information on the depth of the market in each of the member countries.

Table 4.3: Size of the stock market in the member countries

Country	Exchange	No. of companies	Market value of listed companies (£m)
Belgium	Brussels	159	54,318
Denmark	Copenhagen	246	28,587
France	Paris	656	308,750
Germany	Federation of Exchanges	426	313,027
Greece	Athens	150	8,462
Italy	Milan	218	91,888
Luxemburg	Luxemburg	56	13,061
Netherlands	Amsterdam	319	161,084
Portugal	Lisbon	183	2,193
Spain	Madrid	376	99,002
UK	London	1,927	810,102

Source: London Stock Exchange (1994*a*).

It is obvious that a number of the smaller countries have small stock exchanges, in terms of number of companies and market value. Are between 100 and 200 companies representative of a mature economy? Even the German Stock Exchange, which has 460 quoted companies, is still relatively small. Is the estimate of the ERP that is found using historical values of returns from these markets representative? Simply to consider the size of a market may not provide sufficient information on the depth of the market. Two other sets of information are useful: first, the relative size of the stock market to GDP, which is considered in chapter 8, and second, concentration ratios, which are also very important. Table 4.4 provides information on the relative importance of the largest quoted company and the five largest quoted companies in a number of the stock exchanges.

Table 4.4: Concentration ratios for the stock markets

	Percentage of total market value accounted for by:	
Country	**Top company**	**Top 5 companies**
France	4.49	17.20
Germany	7.10	24.84
Italy	12.30	35.95
Netherlands	23.71	44.14
Spain	8.43	30.97
UK	3.61	14.79

Source: London Stock Exchange (1994*a*,*b*).

Table 4.4 shows quite clearly that, for all the markets, the top five companies account for a significant proportion of the total market value. It also shows, however, that, in a number of the smaller exchanges, over a third of the total market value is accounted for by the top five companies. This is bound to have an effect on the ability of any market index to be representative of the true market, let alone all assets, as should be the case with the CAPM.

In relation to the second question, consider the UK. In Tables 4.1 and 4.2, there is good reason for providing cut-off points in 1946 and 1963. The pre- and post-Second World War Stock Exchanges were very different, owing to the rationalisation of industry that took place. The policy of nationalisation and industrial reorganisation changed the composition of the Exchange. Then, in 1963, the FT-A All-share Index was introduced. This was the first attempt at a comprehensive share-price index for the UK and, therefore, marks a clear change in the dataset being considered. It is even possible to argue that the privatisation process of the 1980s and early 1990s has once again changed the composition of the market and a structural break has occurred. If this is true for the third-largest exchange in the world, the problems for smaller exchanges are likely to be even greater.

Alternative approaches

Those problems outlined above and the one outlined below have led to alternative methodologies being proposed for the estimation of the ERP. The final problem is that the figures quoted above are *ex post* rather than *ex ante*. Unanticipated inflation can be expected to erode the value of fixed-interest security returns, while equity returns have greater scope to compensate for unexpected shocks. This means that using *ex post* data provides a misleading estimate of the 'expected' ERP. How can an *ex ante* estimate be derived? A number of approaches have been suggested in various papers. The two that are examined in this sub-section are those of Blanchard (1993) and Jenkinson (1994).

In his 1993 Brookings paper, Blanchard develops two approaches to determining the ERP. First, for the US, UK, Japan, Italy, France and Germany, data is collected from published nominal government Treasury bills or money-market rates—for France and Japan—to provide short-term interest rates, and from longer-dated bonds for an estimate of the medium-term interest rate. Then, estimates of the inflation rate provided by DRI are subtracted to provide estimates of the real interest rate. Appendix 2 contains Blanchard's estimates of the risk-free rate. To verify that this process works, the values derived for the UK are compared to the redemption yields available on index-linked bonds. The results appear to be within an acceptable range. To provide the market return, 'dividend-price' ratios are considered. These are the dividend yields from the various markets. An estimate of the expected growth in dividend prices is then used to derive a return, based on the Gordon growth model. The share is held forever and so no capital gain is ever realised.

Unfortunately, no individual country data is provided in relation to Blanchard's ERP, only a constructed 'world' figure. His result, of a falling ERP, appears to be general across all the markets, but further work would be required to provide individual estimates.

Blanchard's second, and much more complicated approach, is based entirely on US data. Here, *ex post* returns are calculated and regressed against the dataset that could be expected to exist at the time of the investment. This involves the use of various lagged variables, including inflation, realised real rates of capital gain etc. The process is not discussed in detail here, but there are two main conclusions to be drawn from the work. First, the ERP has gone down steadily since the 1950s, although there have been movements above and below the trend line. Second, these transitory increases and decreases appear to be the result of expectations about inflation.

Three further implications are drawn from the work. When the cost of debt and the cost of equity are combined, the overall WACC appears to move less than the two separate elements. This is explained partly by another implication: decreases in the equity premium are likely to translate into both an increase in expected bond rates and a decrease in expected rates of returns on stocks. Finally, although companies that have access to both the equity and bond markets may see little change in their cost of debt, companies relying on debt finance may face a higher cost of capital.

Jenkinson (1994) also considers possible ways of estimating expected inflation at the time of the investment decision. Two more straightforward approaches are used. First, as a bench-mark, it is assumed that investors could accurately predict the long-run rate of inflation and dividend growth over the life of the investment. Second, a prediction of the rates of dividend growth and inflation is derived on an adaptive model with the previous five years' worth of data being employed in the estimation. Exponentially declining weights are employed. The first of these approaches is referred to as Panel A and the second as Panel B. Appendix 3 reports Jenkinson's findings. The crucial importance of this investigation of the UK ERP is that the true figure lies between 4 and 6%, rather than the higher 7–9% traditionally found.

Both papers show the importance of correctly estimating the *ex ante*, rather than the *ex post,* ERP when undertaking this kind of study. They also illustrate another important point: so far no consensus has developed among academics on which estimation process to use, and values therefore vary widely. This is an area where more research is required. There have been quite different approaches to investigating the ERP and these are considered in chapter 5.

Evidence from international studies on the equity risk premium

Only one of the three studies, that of Coopers & Lybrand, considers the question of calculating the ERP by employing the methodology outlined above, although it is a traditional style rather than one of the newer *ex ante* estimates. The EC considers the question but effectively notes simply that the traditional approach is the preferred approach, although inflation raises some problems. The Federal Reserve's method for calculating the cost of equity is discussed in chapter 5.

Coopers & Lybrand calculates an ERP based on an historic average—presumably arithmetic, although this is never stated—over the period 1983–91. The ERP is calculated as the average total return on the equity market, both dividends and capital gain, minus the average short-term money-market rates. The figures are presented in Appendix 1. The fact that certain countries appear to have a higher ERP should not be taken at face value as proof of a higher overall cost of capital. What can be observed for an economy is the cost of equity finance at the average level of gearing for that economy. Gearing is the relationship between the amount of net debt and equity employed by a company. If, on average, companies within a specific country are more highly geared than those in another country, it would not be surprising to see a higher ERP in the more highly geared country. (This depends on the belief that there is an ERP common to all countries. As seen in chapter 2, the fact that equity markets are not yet truly international raises doubts about this proposition.)

Two problems with this approach can be identified. First, although having a consistent time period may be considered valuable for a cross-country survey it would be better to ensure that the best estimate available for each market is used. In the UK this means going back to at least 1963 and probably much further. The same is true of some of the other markets. Second, a different instrument is being employed as the risk-free rate from that used in the earlier part of the paper. Although there may be problems with obtaining inflation estimates for the earlier years in the sample, it would prove better to find the best available for each market. Given the breadth of development of financial markets across the member countries, a strict regime of choosing the 'lowest common denominator' does not have to be employed. Producing best-available estimates for each market should be the aim, especially if a question as vital as that of state aid is being addressed.

Variations in the riskiness of companies across countries

Now that the question of the ERP has been addressed, it is possible to consider the beta estimate. There is much less controversy concerning the calculation of the beta value, although there is also less acceptance of any one 'traditional' approach. The questions concerning the estimation process can be broken down into five main areas. Although these arguments are normally applied to just one market, they are equally applicable to international studies. Each of the five areas is considered in turn.

Before considering these points it is worth investigating the actual meaning of beta. All investments in companies carry two types of risk, that which is specific to the company and that created by general market conditions. Beta is an attempt to measure the relationship between the company and the market, ie the market risk, not the specific risk. There is no reason why investors should be compensated for company-specific risk, as it can be eliminated by holding a diversified portfolio. If investors choose to hold only one type of equity, that is a choice that should have no bearing on the level of return they receive.

Period

Over what period should the calculation occur? There are two conflicting pressures. On the one hand, having the longest-available period ensures that as accurate an estimate as possible is provided. On the other hand, companies are not static. Acquisitions are made, new business activities undertaken and activities divested at a relatively high rate. This means that, over long periods, like-with-like is not being measured and so the value of beta found is not truly representative of the company at that particular point in time. The standard solution applied by the London Business School (LBS) in its Risk Measurement Service is that the last five years of data should be considered. This choice is, however, dependent on the frequency of data which is discussed below. There is no rule that can be applied in this case. The important point is that multiple estimates should be investigated, if it is felt that the company's relationship with the market has been changing over time.

Frequency of observation

There are three options here: daily, weekly or monthly data. Again, each of these will bring differing levels of accuracy but may also be prone to differing levels of statistical noise. If daily data is used, there may be periods when the company and the market move for very different reasons but appear to be highly correlated, either positively or negatively. Effectively, beta measures the correlation between the returns on the market and the company. Some events will therefore have an effect on the value of beta, even though they are not truly related to the market risk of the company. A good example of this is provided by the UK utility companies and political events, especially elections. During the 1992 election, when it appeared that the Labour Party might win, the market fell and the utility companies' share prices plummeted. The reverse happened when the Conservatives won the election. These events should have no bearing on the true beta value, but did lead to a substantial increase in the observed value.

The LBS employs monthly data in its estimates. A better solution is to consider all three options. If each option results in different values, there is obviously something more fundamental which requires investigation.

Bayesian adjustment

In theory, the average beta value for the market should be 1. However, it is often observed that this is not the case. To correct for this problem, an approach called Bayesian adjustment is sometimes used. The adjustment process is as follows:

$$\beta_B = \frac{(\beta_O \times \sigma_O) + (\beta_T \times \sigma_T)}{(\sigma_O + \sigma_T)}$$

where B is the Bayesian adjusted value, *O* is the observed value and *T* is the theoretical value. A weighted average of the beta value is found where the weights are the standard errors of the estimates. It is normal for the theoretical values to be given as 1 and 0.25 for the estimate of beta and its standard error, respectively.

No persuasive evidence has been produced as to why Bayesian adjustment is the correct approach to solving this problem. However, no truly comprehensive attempt at comparing an adjusted and non-adjusted beta estimate in terms of predictive ability has been undertaken.

Non-trading adjustments

In the UK it is often questioned whether the beta values found for those companies that are infrequently traded, primarily those that are members of the unlisted securities market (USM), are correct. This could also be a serious problem in the smaller European exchanges or in those companies that have high levels of share ownership by specific families or institutions, which lead to changes in the small proportion of available equity, causing wild swings in the share price. The worry is that, as the price for these companies changes very infrequently, the relationship between the company's returns and the markets is dominated by periods when nothing happens.

There are two possible solutions. The first is based on the proposition that in market-maker-based exchanges, the price quoted for the company will always be the most up-to-date price, otherwise the market-maker could make a loss, as investors determine that the price is incorrect. Market-makers therefore have every incentive to ensure that the quoted price is changed whenever applicable, rather than just at the time of a trade. This argument may be correct for those markets where an open, quoted-price, market-maker system is employed. Some of the Continental European exchanges do not employ this approach, but use matched-bid systems instead, which could be problematic.

A second solution is based on allowing lags to be employed in the beta estimation process. This then allows changes in the company's share price to be associated with a series of returns from the market. Using this process implies that the market is not efficient and that all values should be calculated in this way. The success of this process in achieving credible results is also unclear.

Competition and the level of beta

An additional complication that should be considered when looking at beta values is the fact that applying the beta value from one company to another may give misleading results owing to the effect of the level of competition. This is especially true of international comparisons, where market conditions can differ substantially.

There is a proposition that the less competitive a market, ie the greater the market power of a company, the lower the company's beta value. This is based on the supposition that a company with market power can pass through the effect of any economic shocks, which would not be possible for companies in a more competitive situation. This insulation from economic shocks means that the returns earned by the company do not vary from those earned in the economy as a whole, hence a lower beta value.

Although the basic premise of this theory is intuitive, several weaknesses can be identified. For the competitive companies to be unable to pass on any cost-shocks to their customers they must face international competition. Otherwise all domestic companies would raise their prices by an equivalent amount to compensate for the cost-shock. Also, the monopolist needs to face an inelastic demand curve, otherwise the impact of passing on the cost-shock would be seen in lower revenue and lower profitability.

In terms of the airline industry this argument may have some validity. Several of the national flag-carriers face little, or no, competition from other airlines in their domestic markets. This could provide a stable base that can be used to pass on cost-shocks. However, it would be wrong to see the whole of the domestic market in this way, as competition exists in the form of alternative modes of transport. There may be specific parts of the market where alternatives are not viable—business travel may be an area where the time saved through air travel makes other forms of transport uncompetitive. Whether or not this has a material impact is unclear, but it does reinforce the need to consider carefully how comparable companies are if a beta value is being inferred from one to another.

Asset betas

Before considering the evidence in relation to beta values there is one final relationship that should be discussed. Problems arise when comparing observed beta values between companies within one country, let alone between countries. This is because the observed value is affected by the company's level of gearing. Normally, the observed value is referred to as the equity beta value. To infer a value for another company, initially the asset beta should be employed and then that company's specific gearing ratio applied, rather than the one of the original comparator company.

Asset betas are found using the following formula:

$$\beta_A = (g \times \beta_D) + [(1-g) \times \beta_E].$$

This relates the asset beta to the gearing level, g, and the equity beta.

Applying CAPM to unlisted companies

Chapter 2 showed quite clearly that the majority of airlines are unlisted, which poses a problem for the preferred approach outlined in the preceding parts of this chapter. There are, however, a number of possible ways around this problem. Although the solution is not perfect, an estimate of the equity cost of capital is possible through the use of a proxy value found from a comparable, quoted company.

Choice of a comparator company

Chapter 2 provided a list of the quoted companies that can be used as comparators for the unlisted companies. The ideal situation is to choose a company from the same country. However, for the vast majority of airlines this is not possible, so comparators from other countries have to be found. To ensure the closest fit, two sets of information are required. First, the spread of geographical business and, second, the split of the types of business should be considered.

The first question relates both to the problem discussed earlier concerning monopoly situations and the impact on beta, and to the broader question of the spreading of risk across many markets. Considering the split of the types of business is also important as non-airlines activities may be included in the group beta value. The split between cargo and passenger and between scheduled and charter will also have an affect on the risk of the company. Whether this risk is relevant to the beta calculation—investors should only be rewarded for market rather than specific risk—does not matter here. Finding the best comparator will ensure that the closest beta value is found.

Decomposition of beta

Having found a quoted comparator company with a beta value it is important to note that the observed beta value is not necessarily the correct value to use. First, adjustments for the financial structure of the company should be made. A process to achieve this, by using asset betas, was outlined above. However, as was mentioned, it is likely that the business split or geographical split of the comparator company will be different. It may be possible to adjust for this also.

Assume that the closest comparator to a state-owned airline is a private company that has three business divisions: air transport, operation of airports and freight distribution by lorry. Then, the observed beta is composed of the following business division betas:

$$\beta_G = \left[\left(\frac{NA_A}{NA_G}\right)\times\beta_A\right]+\left[\left(\frac{NA_P}{NA_G}\right)\times\beta_P\right]+\left[\left(\frac{NA_F}{NA_G}\right)\times\beta_F\right]$$

The subscripts *G*, *A*, *P* and *F* refer to the group, airline division, airport division and freight divisions, respectively. *NA* stands for Net Assets. So, the observed beta for the group is just a weighted average of the betas of the divisions, where the weights are the assets employed in each division as a proportion of the total assets of the group. Asset betas for each division ought really to be found.

In principle, if quoted companies in the other business division areas exist, a beta value for the airline division can be found. This can then be employed as the proxy for the state-owned company's beta value. If the above example were employing UK data, BAA's beta value could be employed for the airport division and that of the National Freight Corporation (NFC) for the freight division. Once asset beta values are known for those companies, the true airline division beta can be found. A numerical example of this methodology is provided in Appendix 4.

Evidence from international studies

None of the three standard international comparisons considers the level of risk associated with a country's exchange, as they are interested in the total market rather than individual companies. There are very few attempts to compare companies across countries. One such study can be used, however, as a lesson in the possible pitfalls.

In 1992 British Gas was referred to the Monopolies and Mergers Commission (MMC) by OFGAS, its regulator. The company also requested a separate referral to the MMC. One of the pieces of information OFGAS had provided in its earlier discussions with the company was the following set of comparative asset betas.

Table 4.5: Asset betas across countries

	UK	France	Germany
Country (all quoted companies)	0.78	0.61	0.42
Water sector	0.57	0.74	0.27
Electricity sector	0.90	0.35	0.44
Gas sector	0.71	n/a	0.44

Source: OFGAS, 1992.

This information was used to infer that the beta value for British Gas's Transportation and Storage division was lower than British Gas's own asset beta—0.65—owing to British Gas being a diversified company. At face value, these figures also appear to be useful in demonstrating that water companies in Germany are much lower risk than those in France or the UK. However, certain questions need to be asked before either of these conclusions can be reached:

- Is the mix of activities and international diversification of that industry the same in each country?
- How are the industries regulated? Comparing UK-style regulation, price regulation, with the US-style, rate-of-return regulation, will provide very different results.

Once these questions have been answered, then the results can be accepted.

Implications for the bench-mark

On a theoretical level, there is no real disagreement that the CAPM is the best-available methodology to estimate the cost of equity. Two components of this methodology are under review, the ERP and the beta estimate.

Traditional estimates of the ERP calculated using *ex post* values of the return on the market and the risk-free rate are being questioned. The risk-free rate is now calculated with an *ex ante* value and this approach should be applied to the ERP also. This raises a problem in terms of how *ex ante* estimates of the return on the market are estimated. A number of methodologies have been proposed; none is perfect but all are preferable to accepting the traditional out-turn figures. Until further academic research is undertaken in this area, the best-available option will be that for which data is available within a country.

With the beta estimate, there is again no right or wrong answer, since academic research has not provided conclusive evidence. The questions of period of data considered and frequency of observations should be answered on a pragmatic basis determined by data availability. Infrequent trading adjustments should be determined according to the market-trading system in place in a specific market. The evidence in support of Bayesian adjustment is inconclusive and, until further research is undertaken, should not be applied to the bench-mark calculation.

A much more serious problem is that of unquoted companies. The majority of member countries have low numbers of quoted companies. This can make finding a comparator to a state-controlled company difficult. Most airlines are state-controlled and the applicability of this bench-mark is, therefore, called into question. Other options, including using international comparators, must be treated carefully owing to the possible differences in the companies. This may be the only course open when undertaking an investigation and so requires further study.

The applicability of the preferred methodology of the CAPM is called into question because of the problems highlighted in this section. It should, however, still be applied using a range of results.

5. ALTERNATIVE APPROACHES TO ESTIMATING THE COST OF CAPITAL

Most emphasis has, until now, been placed on estimating the cost of equity through the CAPM. A number of other approaches, several almost entirely divorced from those mentioned in chapters 3 and 4, are, however, also worth investigating, as they may offer partial solutions to the more intractable problems, caused by data availability, experienced with the application of the preferred methodology. Even if the overall importance of these additional measures is questioned, they can provide corroborative evidence for the estimate of the cost of capital derived from the more formal investigation.

The first two sub-sections consider theoretical alternatives to the CAPM, the dividend growth model (DGM) and the arbitrage pricing theory (APT). Then a number of more general methodologies are considered. Two of these approaches are from specific UK institutions. This may mean their results are of little use in international studies, but it does not necessarily invalidate the methodologies employed.

Dividend growth model

The DGM approach to estimating the cost of equity finance is based on an alternative interpretation of the share price. The value of the equity of a company can be interpreted as the net present value of all future cash streams accruing to the shareholder. Two types of cash stream exist, dividends and the sale value of the equity. If it is assumed that the equity will be held in perpetuity then the only cash stream that matters is the dividend.

Consider the following equation:

$$P_t = \sum_{t=0}^{t=\infty} \left(\frac{D_t}{(1+r)^t} \right).$$

It links the current share price, P, to the flow of discounted dividends, D. These dividends are discounted at the cost of equity, r. As the share is held in perpetuity this simplifies to the sum to infinity of a geometric progression which provides the following equation,

$$P_t = \frac{D_t}{r}.$$

If this equation is rearranged it can be seen that the cost of equity is just the current dividend yield of the company. However, it is overly simplistic to think that the dividend will be unchanging over time, even if real dividends are under consideration. So, the model can be extended to allow for a dividend that grows at a constant rate. Other more complicated versions also exist but the discussion in this book concentrates on the constant growth, or Gordon, model.

If it is known that dividends will grow at a constant rate, say g, per annum, then the first equation can be rewritten as:

$$P_t = \sum_{t=0}^{t=\infty} \left(\frac{D_t (1+g)^t}{(1+r)^t} \right).$$

Again, this summation simplifies:

$$P_t = \frac{D_t (1+g)}{(r-g)}.$$

This can be rearranged as:

$$r = \frac{D_t (1+g)}{P_t} + g.$$

So, the cost of equity finance is the prospective dividend yield plus the expected growth rate.

Although this approach has recently lost popularity to the CAPM, it is still widely employed. Many equity analysts in the UK still use a version of the Gordon model when estimating future share prices. It has also proved to be a popular methodology with several of the regulatory bodies in the UK. The Office of Water Services (OFWAT), the body responsible for the regulation of the water industry, placed great emphasis on this approach in its first consultative paper on the cost of capital in 1992. There are a number of problems with the approach, however, and they are discussed below.

Growth rates

Being required to establish a growth rate for a company's dividend is not straightforward. Although many companies discuss their future dividend strategies in their annual reports, quite general statements are normally made. Even if forecasts are provided, as was the case with GEC in the UK, they cover a relatively short time span, say five years. As discounting is being employed, the values adopted in later years quickly lose their significance. However, a period of more than five years is necessary to provide a reliable estimate of the growth factor and so the cost of equity. In many respects the assumption concerning the growth factor has been the stumbling block for this approach to estimating the cost of capital.

One solution to the problem of forecasting the future dividend growth rate is to use the growth rate that has been achieved by the economy as a whole. This has traditionally been assumed to be about 2% real per annum. Applying that figure allows a 'long-run' cost of equity to be established.

Non-listed companies

As with the preferred option, the CAPM, there is a problem with how to deal with private and state-owned companies. The DGM requires information on the dividend yield, not available for a non-listed company, and the expected dividend growth rate, not necessarily available for this type of company. There are solutions to this problem—employing comparator company information is the most obvious—but they are less than perfect. Where there are no comparators within a country, the use of international comparators is the only possible approach. This is particularly fraught with difficulty owing to the difference in dividend yields that exists between countries. Reasons for this general difference include taxation and share-ownership structures.

Arbitrage pricing theory

A final alternative methodology based on economic theory is that of the APT. This approach can be considered in a number of ways, although one of the standard ways is effectively an extended multi-explanatory variable CAPM rather than a true APT. Consider the equation below:

$$R_e = \alpha + \sum_{i=1}^{i=n} \beta_i x_i .$$

Here, R is the return earned by company e. There are 'n' explanatory factors and each one has an impact of β on that company. Exactly which explanatory factors should be included is an interesting point. This is where the true APT is often corrupted into an extended form of CAPM.

In its pure form, APT does not require the knowledge of the factors that influence the level of return. APT was established as a mechanism for determining the choice of assets to incorporate into a portfolio and so all that is required is the sensitivity to the various factors, the β terms. Knowing these values would allow the establishment of a portfolio that had zero sensitivity to a specific factor, or group of factors. However, this approach is of little use when estimating the level of return for an individual company. Given the question being addressed here, it is probably more relevant to discuss the extended CAPM form of APT. Here, certain explanatory factors assume the role of the theoretical factors discussed in the paragraph above. A typical form the equation can take is given below:

$$R_e = \alpha + (\beta_1 R_m) + (\beta_2 \Delta GDP) + (\beta_3 \Delta r).$$

Here the return on the company is linked to the return on the market, the change in the level of gross domestic product—a proxy for the level of economic activity in an economy—and the change in interest rates—a proxy for the return available elsewhere in the economy. So, this approach bridges the gap between CAPM and APT as multi-explanatory variables are permitted but the factors exist as specific, tangible items rather than nebulous factors.

One of the important problems with this sort of approach is the choice of explanatory variables to include. The variables not only have to be available for forecasting but also the best possible choice of variables has to be made. This is the sticking point: there are numerous possibilities for the explanatory variables and how a final equation is chosen is not straightforward. Those equations that have been proposed have so far proved no better than the standard CAPM at forecasting the level of future returns.

The MMC and rates of return

The MMC plays many roles in the UK. Apart from its position as investigator of mergers and anti-competitive behaviour, it also acts as a court of appeal for the regulated industries. If a regulator and the regulated company cannot agree on the elements of its pricing formula, the MMC can be asked to adjudicate and find a solution. Although this is not the end of an appeal process—a judicial review is the final step after the MMC—a great weight is placed on any decision taken by the MMC.

One set of recommendations that can be seen in this light was that produced in 1993 relating to British Gas. Central to the arguments in this case was the determination of the cost of capital for the Transportation and Storage businesses of the company. The points raised and the evidence sought to corroborate the MMC's preferred solution could have a wider application.

The equity risk premium

Although the MMC claimed explicitly to place little faith in the CAPM, implicit in its calculations is the CAPM formula. The MMC is, however, 'pragmatic' in its use of the methodology and introduced additional ways of establishing the ERP, two of which are worth considering. Both approaches required a mix of traditional and new styles.

First, the ERP was calculated with an historical geometric average of real equity returns—calculated on an *ex post* basis—minus the current real redemption yield on a long-dated index-linked bond. This mix of *ex post* and *ex ante* data was defended on the basis that it was better to be half right than completely wrong. Second, rather than use the *ex post* equity returns data, survey data was employed. Eight fund managers and investors were asked what level of return they expected to earn from a diversified portfolio and whether it was different for utility companies. This information was taken as the market return, from which the redemption yield of the index-linked bond could be subtracted.

Survey data of this kind produces results that are difficult to argue against on an intuitive level. However, the way in which such a survey is undertaken can be the source of debate. Eight is a very small number and there is no information available as to the wording of the question that was asked. If these problems were overcome the results of such a survey would be a very powerful tool in any cost-of-capital determination.

Economy-wide rates of return

Evidence was also sought from an investigation of the out-turn rates of return achieved by the UK economy in general, and the industrial and commercial companies specifically. Current-cost accounting (CCA) information was used, available from the Central Statistical Office (CSO) on a national basis, to overcome the problems of inflation. These actual levels of return were used as a basis for comparison against the real cost of capital.

Undertaking this sort of project raises questions concerning the treatment of depreciation. Specific industries may have very different depreciation systems to those assumed for the national accounts owing to the length of life of assets employed. This will have the effect of raising or lowering the relevant rate of return against which the estimated cost of capital should be measured. Also, no other country in Europe produces CCA information and this approach could not, therefore, be duplicated exactly by other countries.

The Federal Reserve Bank's approach

When estimating the cost of equity finance, the Reserve Bank used a market-calculated ratio as its estimate of the true discount rate. This was the inverse of the price–earnings (PE) ratio—the relationship between the level of profits per share and the price per share in an economy. The inverse of this can be interpreted as a discount rate, or a cost of capital. For example, if Germany had a PE ratio of 12, its cost of equity would be 8.3%.

Some adjustments were made to the basic figure to take into account differences between countries, eg different depreciation schedules. However, several very important differences were not addressed. These are:

- *The composition of the stock market*. If specific types of company dominate a market, a difference in the PE ratios can be expected. The UK has a relatively high number of quoted, high-growth, capital-intensive companies—the biotechnology, computer and pharmaceutical companies—while Germany has a higher proportion of engineering companies quoted. Based on this definition of the cost of equity, the UK is bound to have a lower cost of equity than Germany.

- *The exact definition of profits*. Acceptable accounting practice differs substantially within countries, let alone between countries.

- *The position on the economic cycle*. Share prices are affected by the economic cycle and the impact it has on the expectations of investors. PE ratios should be measured at the same point in the cycle for each country.

These problems are sufficient to mean that little weight can be placed on the use of this methodology when making international comparisons. It may have some relevance when domestic comparisons are being undertaken, but is still not a straightforward methodology to employ. The authors of the Federal Reserve Bank's study list six problems that they are aware of and try to take into account, apart from those given above.

Consumption-time preference

This approach is more firmly rooted in economic theory than financial theory and was proposed in 'Discount Rates and Rates of Return in the Public Sector: Economic Issues' (Spackman, 1991). Although this was primarily concerned with the economic forces that should set public-sector discount factors, the arguments have a relevance to private companies. Of course, as shown in chapter 2, the majority of national flag carriers are still owned by the state.

How should governments set their discount factor? The important question to be addressed is what the time preference for consumers and taxpayers is. As the costs and benefits of any activity undertaken by the state—including nationalised industries—must be assessed, it is this discount factor that should be the baseline. This paper found that a 4–6% range for the real rate of return would be an acceptable estimate. Public investment has an opportunity cost, both through the displacement of consumption—the source of government funds is resources diverted from other parts of the economy, either direct consumption or investment that would yield a flow of future consumption—and the distortionary effects of taxation, and so care needs to be taken in the interpretation of this figure.

A distortionary effect through tax is seen because generally more tax is paid on private financing than public. Primarily, this difference in tax effects is seen through the personal taxes and their interaction with the corporate tax system. The tax wedge between pre-tax and post-tax returns, discussed in detail in the following chapter, should be applied to the government's basic borrowing rate when assessing the public-sector discount factor. If private-sector discount rates are altered for the different risk profiles of private and state projects, a real return of 6% would seem acceptable.

All governments must undertake this kind of investigation at some point. This can be used as a lower bound on the true cost of capital from which the bench-mark for state aid will be assessed. There are difficulties in applying the type of methodology proposed here. However, since it is, at best, supporting evidence for whatever rate has been found by using the preferred methodology, this should not prevent it from being considered.

Implications for the bench-mark

There are different approaches to estimating the cost of capital. Some of them, especially the consumption-time preference and investor surveys, could provide very useful supporting evidence for the more formal, preferred, methodologies set out in chapters 3 and 4. This is of greatest importance to those countries where the formal approaches are difficult to implement. If a range of cost-of-capital estimates is found, because of data problems and the use of comparators, these other approaches can be used to verify that the range is realistic.

6. TAXATION

Once the cost of debt and the cost of equity have been estimated, it is possible to calculate the cost of capital. It is important that the way in which the figure is interpreted is considered very carefully. The cost of capital found is an out-turn amount, the level of return that has to be paid to investors to persuade them to invest in a project. This is not the same as the amount that a company has to earn to be able to pay that level of return, since any income over and above the operating costs of a company may be liable to tax.

When establishing a bench-mark cost of capital for a company, it is the pre-corporate tax figure that is important. To establish this, the individual member country's corporate and personal tax systems need to be investigated. Before a survey of the systems is provided, the theoretical way in which taxation has an impact on the cost of capital will be investigated. As mentioned in chapter 2, this section will draw heavily on the final report of the Ruding Committee.

Throughout the first two sub-sections of this chapter, it will be assumed that companies are in a tax-paying position. The complexities raised by tax exhaustion will be considered alongside leasing in the third sub-section.

Tax structure and the cost of capital

A country's tax system can have an impact on the cost of capital in three ways. First, both the cost of debt and equity can be affected. Finally, the level of investment credits, capital allowances and depreciation systems can have an important effect. Each of these three areas is considered in turn.

Debt

This is the simpler of the two sources of funds to consider from a tax viewpoint. Two possible systems can be operated: either interest payments are tax-deductible, or they are not. If the payments are tax-deductible any taxable profits are reduced by the level of interest payments made by a company. This means that the company does not have to earn a greater level of return to meet its post-corporate-tax cost of debt. Another way of viewing this is that the government, or tax authority, is taxing all profits but then providing a proportion of the interest bill. So, where interest is tax-deductible, the pre- and post-corporate-tax cost of debt is the same. When interest payments are not tax-deductible, the following situation arises:

$$r_d = C_d \times (1 - t_c)$$

or

$$C_d = \frac{r_d}{(1 - t_c)}.$$

If r denotes the post-corporate-tax rate of return, C the pre-tax figure, and t_c is the corporate-tax rate, it can be seen that, for any positive corporate-tax rate, $C > r$. This means that the company has to earn a higher pre-tax rate of return to meet the necessary post-tax cost of debt.

Throughout the EU, the cost of nominal interest payments is tax-deductible. All companies, therefore, face the former rather than the latter situation. Debt will not be considered again until the implications for the cost of capital are assessed.

Equity

Unfortunately the situation is not as straightforward for equity finance. The only part of the total return that a company has any control over is the dividend payment—the income return associated with an investor's funds. Dividends are always paid out of post-corporate-tax profits. Yet again, two possible approaches exist, although, as is seen later, these actually set the bounds for a myriad of possibilities.

First, there is the 'classical' system. In this, the tax paid by the company is treated as any normal tax payment. The resulting funds can then be used by a company as it sees fit. Paying dividends is obviously one available option, as is investing the funds in the company's activities. The shareholder who then receives the dividend payment is liable to personal income tax. Within the classical system, this creates the double-taxation of dividends, both the company and the investor are liable to tax.

In terms of the returns framework developed above, the relationship in a classical system is:

$$r_e = C_e \times (1 - t_c)$$

or

$$C_e = \frac{r_e}{(1 - t_c)}.$$

Therefore, there is no difference to the non-deductible interest-payment option above. A higher rate of return must be earned to meet the required post-corporate-tax cost of equity.

There is a second option, the 'imputation' system of taxation. This approach is an attempt to allow for the double-taxation of dividends. Although the company still has to pay corporation tax on its distributed profits, part or all of the tax is then given as a tax credit to the shareholders to cover their personal income-tax liability. So, the effective cost of equity capital is different, as the shareholders, the owners of the company, face a lower overall tax bill:

$$r_e = C_e \times \frac{(1-t_c)}{(1-t_i)}$$

or

$$C_e = \frac{r_e(1-t_i)}{(1-t_c)}.$$

According to the actual system of tax operated in a country, there may be specific factors which subsequently alter the overall impact. Examples of this are setting the imputation rate equal to the basic rate of income tax and creating time distortions in the payment of tax on dividends and tax on undistributed profits. However, these do not detract from the overall influence of this choice of system which is that, provided that the imputation rate is positive, the level of pre-tax returns a company has to earn is lower than that under a classical system.

Capital allowances
Apart from the direct impact on each of the forms of finance, there is another way in which taxation can alter the cost of capital. This is through the additional benefits available, as depreciation allowances and capital allowances. These lower the cost of capital in as much as the level of taxable profits is altered. There is a way of building these influences into the cost-of-capital equation, although it is complicated. Very good explanations of different approaches to their incorporation are provided by the OFWAT and Water Services Association (WSA) papers on the cost of capital (OFWAT, 1991; WSA, 1991).

A framework for establishing the impact

Having determined that the corporate tax system can have an impact on the cost of capital, it is necessary to develop a framework within which these influences can be assessed. Possibly the most generally accepted, although not the only approach is that provided by King and Fullerton (1984), which has been subsequently implemented and broadened—in terms of countries covered—by the Organisation for Economic Cooperation and Development (OECD) and the Ruding Committee. This approach employs the methodologies developed above, but also incorporates the impact of the capital allowances and depreciation allowances. To assess how these tax rules affect the cost of capital, the sources of investment funds are included. These are taken as the marginal sources rather than the average, since this methodology is interested in the marginal effect of taxation. These flows are considered in detail in chapter 7.

For the King–Fullerton approach, it is important to have a common base rate against which the different countries' tax regimes can be assessed. In the standard approach adopted, a real rate of return of 5% demanded by investors—pre-investor tax but post-corporate tax—is assumed on all assets across all countries. This is obviously a gross simplification but makes comparison of corporate tax wedges—the difference between the pre- and post-tax costs—easy.

The tax regimes
Before considering the impact of taxation, it is necessary to consider the actual tax regimes in place across the member countries. Table 6.1 summarises this information.

Table 6.1: Corporate tax system and statutory rates (1991)

Country	Type of system	Overall tax rate[1] (%)	Imputation rate[2] (%)
Belgium[3]	modified classical	39	0
Denmark	modified classical	38	0
France	partial imputation	34	33.3
		42[4]	
Germany	full imputation and	57.5	36
	split-rate method	45.6	
Greece	zero-rate method	46[5]	0
Ireland	partial imputation	43/10[6]	5.5
Italy	full imputation	47.83	36
Luxemburg	unmodified classical	39.39	0
Netherlands	unmodified classical	35	0
Portugal	modified classical	39.6	0
Spain	dividend reduction	35.34	0
UK[3]	partial imputation	34	25

Notes:
[1] In most cases, the overall tax rate differs from simple addition of the rates at each level of tax authority—state or local government—because intermediate or local rates may be either deducted in computing central government taxes or calculated on a different base.
[2] As a proportion of gross dividend.
[3] These countries apply lower rates to corporations with profits below a certain threshold.
[4] On distributed profits (34% since January 1st 1992).
[5] Varies with activity, status and nature of investment.
[6] 10% manufacturing sector and certain services, otherwise 43%.
Source: Ruding Committee (1992).

As can be seen, there is a wide spread between the classical approach and the imputation approach. This is bound to have an effect on the tax wedges. No attempt has been made to summarise the depreciation allowances. Information on these can be found in the Ruding Committee report.

The impact of tax on the cost of capital

Table 6.2 summarises the results of the fixed 5% rate-of-return application of the King–Fullerton methodology by the Ruding Committee.

Table 6.2: Cost of capital for domestic investment, % (1)

	Average for each type of asset			Average for each source of finance			Overall average	Standard deviation
Country	**B**	**M**	**I**	**Retained earnings**	**New shares**	**Debt**		
Belgium	5.4	4.2	8.3	6.9	6.9	2.8	5.4	2.5
Denmark	6.0	5.3	6.8	7.2	7.2	3.2	5.8	2.0
France	5.4	4.6	7.3	7.0	3.5	3.5	5.4	2.1
Germany	5.1	5.2	6.9	8.8	2.2	1.4	5.6	3.8
Greece	5.0	4.8	5.9	7.1	2.7	2.7	5.1	2.2
Ireland	4.9	5.0	5.5	5.4	5.0	4.6	5.1	0.5
Italy	6.7	5.5	6.3	8.8	2.6	2.6	6.0	3.1
Luxemburg	6.9	4.9	8.4	7.8	7.8	3.4	6.2	2.5
Netherlands	6.0	5.2	6.2	7.0	7.0	3.2	5.7	1.8
Portugal	6.1	5.2	6.4	7.3	7.3	2.9	5.7	2.2
Spain	5.7	5.5	7.9	7.5	7.5	3.5	6.1	2.1
UK	5.8	5.2	7.4	7.4	4.7	3.7	5.9	1.9

Notes: B = buildings; M = machinery; I = inventories. Based on the following assumptions: no personal taxes, 3.1% inflation, average weights.
Source: Ruding Committee (1992).

Table 6.2 presents scenarios for three types of asset and three sources of finance. When the types of assets are considered, the source of finance is assumed to be the relevant national mix of the three available types.

Each of these rates of return should be seen as the pre-corporate-tax cost of capital required in that country. To assess the impact of the tax system, therefore, the figures should be compared to the assumed 5% post-tax required rate. For the UK this shows that the tax system penalises retained earnings above all other forms of finance, and inventories above all other assets. The overall average can be used to assess the total impact of the tax system. Companies in Luxemburg face the greatest wedge and consequently have to earn the highest pre-tax rate of return, based on these figures. Companies in Greece and Ireland face the smallest tax wedge. These tax wedges are set out in Table 6.3.

Table 6.4 contains the results of applying this methodology to the countries still using the 5% real rate of return, but removing the assumption of common inflation rates.

Table 6.3: Corporate tax wedges for domestic investment

	Average for each type of asset			Average for each source of finance			Overall average	Standard deviation
Country	**B**	**M**	**I**	**Retained earnings**	**New shares**	**Debt**		
Belgium	0.4	–0.8	3.3	1.9	1.9	–2.2	0.4	2.5
Denmark	1.0	0.3	1.8	2.2	2.2	–1.8	0.8	2.0
France	0.4	–0.4	2.3	2.0	–1.5	–1.5	0.4	2.1
Germany	0.1	0.2	1.9	3.8	–2.8	–3.6	0.6	3.8
Greece	0.0	–0.2	0.9	2.1	–2.3	–2.3	0.1	2.2
Ireland	–0.1	0.0	0.5	0.4	0.0	–0.4	0.1	0.5
Italy	1.7	0.5	1.3	3.8	–2.4	–2.4	1.0	3.1
Luxemburg	1.9	–0.1	3.4	2.8	2.8	–1.6	1.2	2.5
Netherlands	1.0	0.2	1.2	2.0	2.0	–1.8	0.7	1.8
Portugal	1.1	0.2	1.4	2.3	2.3	–2.1	0.7	2.2
Spain	0.7	0.5	2.9	2.5	2.5	–1.5	1.1	2.1
UK	0.8	0.2	2.4	2.4	–0.3	–1.3	0.9	1.9

Notes: B = buildings; M = machinery; I = inventories. These wedges represent the difference between the cost of capital reported in Table 6.2 and 5%.
Source: Ruding Committee (1992).

Table 6.4: Cost of capital for domestic investment, % (2)

	Average for each type of asset			Average for each type of finance			Overall average	Standard deviation
Country	**B**	**M**	**I**	**Retained earnings**	**New shares**	**Debt**		
Belgium	5.7	4.5	8.8	9.3	9.3	4.2	6.4	3.1
Denmark	6.9	6.1	7.6	10.2	10.2	5.1	6.9	2.5
France	6.4	5.4	8.3	9.3	4.9	5.0	6.3	2.3
Germany	4.8	4.9	6.4	10.2	2.6	1.6	5.3	4.3
Ireland	6.0	6.2	6.7	6.6	6.0	5.6	6.2	0.5
Italy	7.7	6.8	6.7	11.3	1.8	1.8	7.0	4.7
Netherlands	7.5	6.5	7.9	8.6	8.6	4.5	7.0	2.1
Portugal	2.5	2.4	1.2	5.9	5.9	–1.4	2.3	3.7
UK	5.2	4.8	7.7	6.6	3.4	2.3	5.6	2.1

Note: B = buildings; M = machinery; I = inventories. In the calculations the following information was used: country-specific inflation rates, actual interest rates and country-specific weights. No personal taxes are considered and only countries with data on weights are included.
Source: Ruding Committee (1992).

Table 6.4 shows clearly that, when more actual information is included, the picture becomes less uniform. Portugal has a negative tax impact, possibly because of the high inflation and high actual interest rates. Of those countries where it is possible to undertake this more realistic simulation, three separate groups can be found. The low-tax countries are Portugal, Germany and the UK, medium-tax are Ireland, France and Belgium and high-tax are Denmark, Italy and The Netherlands. The information on specific types of finance is returned to in chapter 7.

Of the international studies, the only one worth considering here is the Coopers & Lybrand report. The ranking of absolute tax wedges is different from that found by the Ruding Committee. Table 6.5 provides the information on tax on a comparative basis.

Table 6.5: Comparative effects of the tax regime

	Tax wedge as a % of post-tax cost of capital	
Country	**Ruding Committee**	**Coopers & Lybrand**
Belgium	28.0	16.9
Denmark	38.0	11.9
France	6.0	9.9
Germany	26.0	38.9
Ireland	26.0	5.4
Italy	24.0	35.8
Netherlands	40.0	29.1
Portugal	–54.0	18.9
UK	12.0	39.9

Source: Ruding Committee (1992), Coopers & Lybrand.

Table 6.5 serves to illustrate two points. The first is that, although some countries have high absolute tax wedges, part of this is the result of a high cost of capital. Once a proportionate tax wedge has been calculated, a new ranking should be constructed. Second, the two studies present very different results. The reasons for this should be investigated further. However, the Ruding Committee figures will be taken as the correct ones on the grounds that the study was interested in taxation, only, rather than the wider cost-of-capital question. Importantly, both studies used the King–Fullerton approach, which is our preferred approach.

Leasing

Often associated with the question of tax exhaustion and the impact of corporate tax systems on investment policy is the question of leasing.

Leasing developed owing to the profitability of financial institutions and the tax exhaustion of industrial and commercial companies. Before considering the leasing system, tax exhaustion should be investigated. This can occur for two reasons. Either companies make a trading loss, so giving rise to no taxable profits, or companies are undertaking high levels of investment and find that the stock of tax credits from capital allowances and interest deductions are greater than the level of profits. This creates problems through an alteration of the tax wedge. In the UK, for example, advance corporation tax (ACT), the imputation tax on dividends, has to be paid whether or not a company is tax-exhausted. This means that the cost of capital for the company is altered. This problem should be dealt with on a case-by-case basis when the cost of capital is being calculated.

Leasing helps solve this problem by the financial institution acquiring an asset which it then provides to another company to use in return for a rental payment. The financial institution can lower its taxable profits, through the capital allowances, and the tax-exhausted company can be given access to assets at a cheaper rate than if they were acquired outright. This last part arises because the company which cannot make use of the capital allowances is given some of the benefits the financial institution derives from its use of the allowances.

Two types of lease exist, operating and financial. With an operating lease the lessor is often responsible for maintenance and upkeep of the asset and sometimes clauses covering obsolescence are included. With a financial lease the lessee has much greater responsibility for the asset, often to the point of being able to acquire the asset at the end of the lease for a relatively small payment. Fixed assets are usually financed through finance leases while other perishable assets, such as computers and vehicles, are normally leased through operating leases. One way of defining the type of lease that is being entered into is to look at the accrual of net present value benefits. If 90% or more accrue to the lessee a lease is deemed to be a finance rather than an operating lease. Finance leases are shown on the balance sheet and treated like debt finance in many respects. Effectively, the substance rather than the form is the determining factor; if most of the risks and rewards of ownership are transferred to the lessee it is classified as a finance lease. All countries should follow this classification approach as it is enshrined in International Accounting Standard 17.

Although there have been changes in the tax and accounting treatment of leases, especially in the UK, they are still an important source of finance, as illustrated in Table 6.6.

Leasing is a viable source of finance, even without the tax advantages, for several other reasons, such as:

- *Flexibility*. Leases often allow flexibility in two ways. Seasonal industries can load their payments on to the high cash-flow part of their year, which is especially important for airlines. If technology is changing rapidly, as in the computer industry, to purchase an expensive piece of hardware that could become obsolete before the end of its actual life is impractical, especially if the option of leasing is available. Lessors are often willing to build in obsolescence clauses that allow assets to be exchanged. This is especially true of manufacturers that act as lessors.

Table 6.6: New investment leasing finance

Country	1989 (ECU m)	Leasing as a % of global investments in 1989
Belgium	1,323	8.3
Denmark	779	4.5
France	21,789	19.7
Germany	9,911	17.8
Greece	110	1.2
Italy	8,328	14.7
Ireland	789	28.4
Luxemburg	161	9.0
Netherlands	2,312	17.4
Portugal	804	7.2
Spain	8,933	27.0
UK	20,161	30.1

Source: European Commission (1991/92).

- *No capital expenditure*. As the lessee does not have to acquire the asset, it does not have to finance an acquisition. For governments with budget deficits, this may prove an attractive option, especially for expensive items such as aircraft.

- *Maintenance*. As mentioned earlier, with an operating lease the lessor takes much of the responsibility for the maintenance of the asset. This removes the need for a company to hire specialist workers or pay third parties to undertake the activity.

It is quite obvious that leasing is a popular form of finance for airlines. GPA, an Irish company, was the largest aircraft-leasing company in the world prior to its financial difficulties in the early 1990s. At one point, it was responsible for the acquisition of over two-thirds of the aircraft produced in Western Europe and America. Even BA, the most profitable European airline and the one with the greatest access to the financial markets, had 69 aircraft on operating leases in 1992. This was 30% of its total fleet.

An understanding of the leasing market is essential, when establishing the cost of finance for an airline. However, as the majority of leases are contracted with an Irish company, in principle, the determining factor is the cost of finance in Ireland, as GPA needs to finance its own operations. Unless there are specific factors driving the cost of capital for leases in that country, it should probably be the case that the cost of capital there should be included in the bench-mark figure for the individual company. Lease-rental payments are treated in the same way as interest payments; they can be deducted from taxable profits and so leasing is a specific form of debt.

Implications for the bench-mark

Taxation is an important consideration when comparing the cost of capital between countries. The interaction between the corporate and personal income-tax systems is very important. Throughout Europe, all the possible corporation-tax systems exist, ranging from classical to full imputation.

The effect of taxation is assessed in a relatively straightforward way. Airlines, however, pose a problem because of the level of losses that they have made over the past decade. There are solutions to the problem of tax exhaustion, but they can make the calculation of the tax wedge much more complicated.

7. FINANCING PROPORTIONS

Having discussed the cost of each type of finance, and the implication for each from the tax system operating within a country, it is now necessary to determine how to bring the information together into one bench-mark cost of capital. The traditional measure of this is the WACC. This employs the gearing ratio—debt as a proportion of the total capital employed. When the gearing ratio is included, an average cost of capital is estimated. However, there are two reasons why this might not be an appropriate measure. First, measuring the capital stock is not an easy process owing to differences in accounting practice, especially depreciation policy. Second, it is an historical measure. More pertinent to the question under consideration is the answer to the following question, 'If a company were to raise finance for a project today, what proportions of debt and equity would it employ?' This is a consideration of the source of marginal financing and as such requires flow-of-funds information.

As the aim of this book is to provide a methodology for establishing a bench-mark cost of capital, the relationship between the average and the marginal costs of capital should be mentioned. It is likely that the marginal cost of capital will be greater than the average. If a project passes a bench-mark test at the marginal cost of capital, it is likely that it would also pass one at the average cost of capital.

We begin by discussing the various sources of finance available to a company. We then consider two possible ways of measuring these sources and the implications of using each of them. The available evidence on the international differences in the flow of funds is investigated, at both a national economy level and at a quoted company level. We then consider the more traditional approach of gearing and assesses its relevance when making international studies. Finally, we consider the implications for the cost of capital.

Sources of finance

Apart from debt and equity finance, there are another four sources that are typically considered and these are discussed below.

- *Internally generated funds*. These are the profits earned by the company and retained within it for internal investment purposes, rather than distributed as dividends to the shareholders.

- *Bank finance*. As its name suggests, this is the amount of debt finance raised from bank sources in the form of term loans and overdrafts.

- *Trade credit*. At a national level, this should be interpreted as either the amount of prepayment for goods and services the industrial and commercial sector receives from the other sectors in an economy—households, financial institutions, the state and the overseas sector—or the amount of goods and services this sector receives from these other sectors that have not yet been paid for. When different sizes of company are considered, the definition has to be widened to include the same items mentioned above, but coming from companies in the different size categories.

- *Capital transfers*. These are local, national and transnational government grants to industry. An example of this in the UK would be special development area grants.

Gross and net definitions

Exactly what should be valued in the flow-of-funds calculation? There are two possible answers to this and the way in which the information is interpreted depends critically on which definition is chosen.

The gross flow of funds answers the question, 'Irrespective of the use made of the funds, what proportion of each type of finance did a company raise?' A net definition is concerned much more with the use to which the funds are put. It is an accounting relationship that states that the total net funds raised must equal the investment in physical assets undertaken by a company or country. Consider the following simplified example.

> *A company raises £200m of equity finance and £100m of debt finance in a year. Of this, £50m is used to acquire the equity of another company, £30m is used to repay a term loan with a bank and £220m worth of machinery is acquired.*

In this example the total gross flow of funds is £300m, split 67% equity/33% debt. However, if the equity acquired is netted off the equity finance raised, and the debt repaid is subtracted from the new debt finance, the net flow of funds is found. This totals £220m, of which £150m (68%) is equity and £70m (32%) is debt. So, this is an important consideration, especially in those countries where equity markets are developed, since the market is both a source of finance and a place where the control of companies can be bought and sold. Where possible, the net flow of funds will be considered, as this provides a greater insight into the true financing decisions of actual investment than the gross funds can.

Evidence on the flow of funds

A number of studies have investigated the flow of funds in various countries. Some have concentrated at the national macroeconomic level, while others have considered more specific groups of companies, selected according either to the sector to which they belong or to some size category. There are also two sources of information from which these flows can be constructed. Individual company accounting information can be aggregated, or national information collected by government departments can be used.

National level data

Tables 7.1 and 7.2 consider information for the UK, Germany, Japan and the US on both gross and net definitions. The figures relate to a weighted average where the weights are the capital goods price index in each year and the level of total investment.

Table 7.1: Gross sources of finance % (1970–89)

Source of finance	Germany	Japan	UK	US
Internal	62.4	40.0	60.4	62.7
Bank finance	18.0	34.5	23.3	14.7
Bonds	0.9	3.9	2.3	12.8
New equity	2.3	3.9	7.0	–4.9
Trade credit	1.8	15.6	1.9	8.8
Capital transfers	6.6	–	2.3	–
Other	8.0	2.1	2.9	5.9

Source: Corbett and Jenkinson (1993).

A negative value for the gross equity source of funds exists for the US since gross sources are reported net of purchases.

Table 7.2: Net sources of finance % (1970–89)

Source of finance	Germany	Japan	UK	US
Internal	80.6	69.3	97.3	91.3
Bank Finance	11.0	30.5	19.5	16.6
Bonds	–0.6	4.7	3.5	17.1
New equity	–0.9	3.7	–10.4	–8.8
Trade credit	–1.9	–8.1	–1.4	–3.7
Capital Transfers	8.5	–	2.5	–
Other	1.5	–0.1	–2.9	–3.8
Statistical adjustment	0.0	0.0	–8.0	–8.7

Source: Corbett and Jenkinson (1993).

Other researchers have expanded the number of countries considered but have not considered as long a time-frame. Work by Mayer (1990) considers a larger number of European countries but only over the period 1970–85. Although the same sort of weighted average was calculated, it was not available for all countries and only a simple average is provided in Table 7.3. To provide the best-possible comparison, the figures for the UK and Germany have been reproduced alongside those of Finland, France and Italy. Only the net figures are given here.

Table 7.3: Unweighted average net financing of non-financial enterprises (1970–85)

Type of finance	UK	Germany	Finland	France	Italy
Retentions	102.4	70.9	64.4	61.4	51.9
Capital transfers	4.1	8.6	0.2	2.0	7.7
Short-term securities	1.7	–0.1	3.7	–0.1	–1.3
Loans	7.6	12.1	28.1	37.3	27.7
Trade credit	–1.1	–2.1	–1.4	–0.6	0.0
Bonds	–1.1	–1.0	2.8	1.6	1.6
Shares	–3.3	0.6	–0.1	6.3	8.2
Other	3.2	10.9	7.4	–1.4	1.0
Statistical adjustment	–13.4	0.0	–5.0	–6.4	3.2

Source: Mayer (1990)

Information was also provided by the Ruding Committee on this. Table 6.4 used the actual flow-of-funds information when establishing the marginal cost of capital tax wedge. Information provided in Table 7.4 is more simplified than that provided in Table 7.3 and was taken from an earlier OECD study. It does appear to be net flows though, rather than gross. Table 7.4 reproduces the information employed by the Ruding Committee.

Table 7.4: Proportion of total investment

Country	Retained earnings	New equity	Debt
Belgium	0.23	0.21	0.56
Denmark	0.20	0.15	0.65
France	0.30	0.11	0.59
Germany	0.42	0.08	0.50
Ireland	0.79	0.08	0.13
Netherlands	0.55	0.06	0.39
Portugal	0.47	0.03	0.50
UK	0.73	0.10	0.17

Source: Ruding Committee (1992).

These figures appear quite different from those presented in the Tables 7.1–7.3 and so require further investigation. They do, however, provide information for a number of other countries, outside the scope of the earlier tables, and so are a useful source of additional information.

Specific groups of companies

Although the information on the whole economy provides much that is useful, it is equally important to consider the flow of funds to quoted companies. As shown in chapter 4, the importance of the quoted sector differs from country to country and it is important, therefore, to investigate how quoted companies finance themselves. Mayer and Alexander (1990) consider information on large and medium-sized quoted companies in London and Frankfurt. Table 7.5 sets out their findings. The investigation covered the period 1982–86.

Table 7.5: Gross and net sources of finance in Germany and the UK, % (1982–88)

	Gross		Net	
Type of finance	**Germany**	**UK**	**Germany**	**UK**
Retentions	89.6	58.2	137.9	112.9
New equity	8.2	14.3	–10.2	–11.3
Medium-/long-term loans	0.6	7.9	8.8	14.1
Short-term loans	–1.7	1.1	–4.0	–25.6
Trade credit	3.3	18.5	–32.6	9.9

Source: Mayer and Alexander (1990).

Interpretation of the results

Surprisingly, on a net basis, none of the countries raises a significant proportion of its finance from the stock market. The reason for this was given earlier. It is the stock market's second function, that of the market for corporate control, that dominates on a national level. For individual companies, especially smaller companies, the market can be an important source of funds, but not at an aggregate level. Just as important is the fact that retained earnings are the single most important source of finance for any of the countries considered. This is not borne out by the Ruding Committee work but, as mentioned before, those results must be treated carefully.

Gearing and capital structure

The preceding sub-sections of this chapter have been concerned with one approach to measuring the capital structure of a company. However, it is not the traditional approach adopted in the estimation of the cost of capital. Rather than use a flow value, as described in above, it is traditional to use a stock value, gearing. It has been mentioned several times already in this book without being fully explained. This section considers the available definitions of gearing, its measurement, empirical studies into gearing levels and the relative accuracy of gearing compared to a flow figure.

Gearing is concerned with the measurement of the relative importance of debt and equity in the company's financial structure.

Definitions of gearing

While numerous definitions of gearing exist, only the most important ones are considered in this book. There are two types of definition: the first is concerned with the definition of the denominator while the second is concerned with the measurement of the constituent parts of the equation. If the first set of definitions is considered, two options exist. Either debt can be measured relative to equity, the first equation below, or it can be measured relative to the total capital employed—the sum of debt and equity—given in the second equation:

$$G = \frac{D}{E} \tag{1}$$

$$G = \frac{D}{(D + E)} \tag{2}$$

Of these, equation 2 is the preferred definition and is employed in the calculation of asset betas, etc, as detailed earlier. The debt figure employed should be the net debt, not the gross debt of the company. If gross debt is employed, misleading figures could occur as some companies hold high debt levels and correspondingly high liquid assets. Also, when making international comparisons it is important to control for the differing levels of cash balance required by banks in different countries, which is achieved by using net debt.

Having established a preferred form for the measure, the definition of the individual constituents of the figure must be considered. Again, there are two basic options. Either book values of debt and equity can be employed or market values. Book values have an advantage in as much as they are available for all companies. However, book values may be misleading for two different reasons. First, the 'true' value of the company is more accurately given by the market value than the book value when historic-cost accounting is employed. Unless current-cost accounting information is available for all companies, the values found may not be representative. Second, different countries have different depreciation regimes, which will have an impact on the book value shown in the accounts. So like may not be compared with like.

It would appear, then, that market values are the solution. Yet, problems are again encountered. As has been mentioned several times, the majority of airlines, like the vast majority of companies, are not quoted. So, market values of equity are not available. Even for those companies that are quoted, the majority of their debt will not be quoted. This provides problems with adopting this approach. The preferred options become:

- market value of debt and equity;
- book value of debt and market value of equity;
- book value of debt and equity.

There are ways in which the market-value figures can be proxied, but they are unreliable and potential minefields of problems when making international comparisons.

Empirical evidence of gearing figures

Each of the three principal international studies adopts a different approach to defining and measuring the gearing ratio. Coopers & Lybrand, whose figures are reproduced in Appendix 1, employs a book-value version of equation 1. This explains why figures in excess of one can be found for the ratio. The EC study also employs historic-cost data, but on the basis of equation 2. Finally, the Federal Reserve Bank study employs a mixture of the book value of debt and the market value of equity, but with an equation 1 definition. So there is no consistent approach in these studies.

Gearing and tax effects

One point that should be stressed in relation to gearing is that it has two possible additional impacts on the cost of capital. First, gearing affects the equity beta value and, therefore, the cost of capital. This result is implicitly discussed in chapter 4, when asset betas are explained. There is a fundamental question concerned with the zero value assigned to the debt beta, which has not been investigated in this book. Owing to the importance of debt finance to the airline industry and the possible significant impact non-zero debt betas could have on the cost of capital, it is an area that requires further research.

Second, high levels of gearing are often associated with companies that are tax-exhausted. This ties in with the discussion of tax exhaustion arising from interest-payment deductibility set out in chapter 6.

Problems associated with the use of gearing

Several of the problems with the use of gearing have already been identified. Primarily, the fact that stock figures are not measured on a consistent basis between countries and that differential inflation rates exist, are problems that make the use of gearing figures difficult. There is also a more fundamental problem. As gearing is a stock measure, it is an historic figure that may have little to do with the future mix of debt and equity that a company wishes to employ. This could lead to misleading figures being found.

One way of checking whether companies are sticking to their historic capital structure or whether it is changing is to consider the flow-of-funds information provided earlier. If it proves to be the case that a significantly different flow figure exists, then it is this figure that should be used. Of course, using the flow figures the whole time meets this criterion and ensures that some of the other problems with stock figures are also avoided.

Implications for the cost of capital

When calculating the WACC for a company based on the simplified version of the flow-of-funds data, the following formula should be applied:

$$\text{WACC} = (C_e \times E) + (C_R \times R) + (C_d \times D).$$

R denotes retained profits, E is new equity and D is debt. Each is measured as the proportion of physical investment financed through that type of funds. A different pre-tax cost of capital is required to achieve the desired post-tax cost of capital. This is just a more advanced version of the standard WACC calculation.

Retained profits should be treated as a form of internal equity finance, but must be separated from external equity owing to the different tax treatment. The reason retained profits are treated in this way is because they form part of distributable profits. Companies have several choices as to how they employ post-interest and post-tax profits. Dividends can be paid or the money can be invested in the company, say through the purchase of new fixed assets. The retained profits are therefore shareholder funds that have not been taken out of the company but are still 'owned' by the shareholders, hence their treatment as equity.

8. RELEVANCE OF INSTITUTIONAL DIFFERENCES

Now that the basic bench-mark cost-of-capital model has been developed, a number of potential problem areas need to be considered. The first part of this chapter concentrates on the relative importance of various financial institutions in each of the countries, while the later part investigates whether there are differences in the practices of these institutions.

Chapter 7 highlighted several points concerning the importance of different institutions as a source of finance. Here, the investigation will be taken further, with the central theme being the implications for the cost of capital arising from these differences.

Importance of the stock market

There are a number of ways of assessing the relative importance of the stock market across countries. Tables 4.3 and 4.4 provided some evidence on the relative importance of stock markets between countries. One further measure that can be used is to compare the total market value of an exchange to the level of GDP in a country. Although this measure is far from perfect—a stock figure is being compared with a flow figure—it is the best that is available across many countries. It provides different information to the tables in chapter 4, in as much as the data has now been 'normalised' through comparison to a measure of the size of an economy. Table 8.1 combines the information from Table 4.3 and the latest nominal GDP figures—1993 for all countries apart from Belgium and Portugal, where 1992 data are used—to provide this comparative measure.

Table 8.1 provides a clear indication of the traditional split between the UK and Continental Europe. It would be reinforced if the other Anglo-Saxon economy, the US, were included. In the UK the market has much greater significance than in other European countries. There are, however, quite clear splits even within Continental Europe. A number of countries, especially The Netherlands and, to a certain extent, Belgium and France, have relatively important stock exchanges. There are also three countries where the stock market has little importance, Greece, Portugal and Italy. Many reasons can be suggested for this, including the attitudes of different investor groups and the ownership structure of the corporate sector. These will have an influence on the cost of capital and are investigated in the following sub-sections.

Table 8.1: Relative importance of the stock market (£ billion)

Country	Market value of listed companies	Nominal GDP	Market value as a % of GDP
Belgium	54.3	145.8	37.2
Denmark	28.6	90.1	31.7
France	308.8	835.6	37.0
Germany	313.0	1,144.2	27.4
Greece	8.5	49.2	17.3
Italy	91.9	638.4	14.4
Netherlands	161.1	204.9	78.6
Portugal	2.2	56.1	3.9
Spain	99.0	318.9	31.0
UK	810.1	627.1	129.2

Note: The market value figures relate to the market value of domestic companies, not all quoted companies.
Source: GDP estimates, *Consensus Forecasts* (1994), author's calculations.

Shareholder profiles across countries

Even when the overall importance of a stock market has been assessed, there is still a secondary question concerning who the investors are. The implications of the shareholder profiles are discussed in the next sub-section. It can help to explain why the importance of stock markets varies between countries. It is an area where high quality data is not easily available, although it is possible to infer the importance of various shareholder categories from pieces of secondary evidence. Certain categories of shareholder are easier to identify than others. Evidence relating to the most important ones is considered here.

UK and German evidence

There is a long history of detailed surveys of shareholders in the UK, undertaken by either the CSO or the London Stock Exchange. The results of these surveys are presented in Table 8.2.

The importance of direct individual investment has fallen since the 1960s, although the 1980s and early 1990s see a stabilisation as a result of the privatisation issues. Pension funds and other financial institutions have become much more important over this time. These are effectively indirect individual holdings, although there are tax differences that mean this change in investment vehicle has an important effect on corporate policy.

There is also a source of detailed evidence concerning share ownership in Germany. Table 8.3 reproduces data available for 1984 and 1988.

Table 8.2: Percentage of UK quoted securities owned by various sectors

Shareholder category	1963	1981	1989	1992
Personal	54.0	28.2	20.6	21.3
Pension funds	6.4	26.7	30.5	34.7
Insurance companies	10.0	20.5	18.5	16.5
Investment trusts	11.3	5.4	1.6	2.1
Other financial institutions	–	1.4	1.5	0.9
Unit trusts	1.3	3.6	5.9	6.2
Charities	2.1	2.2	2.3	1.8
Banks	1.3	0.3	0.7	0.5
Industrial and commercial companies	5.1	5.1	3.8	1.7
Public sector	1.5	3.0	2.0	1.5
Overseas holders	7.0	3.6	12.7	12.8

Table 8.3: Ownership of shares issued by German enterprises (%)

Ownership of shares	1984	1988
Private individuals	18.8	19.7
Non-financial enterprises	36.1	39.1
Banks	7.6	8.1
Investment funds	2.7	3.5
Insurance enterprises	3.1	2.7
Government	10.2	7.0
Foreigners	21.4	20.0

Note: Insurance companies are excluded.
Source: Supplement to the Monthly Report of the Deutsche Bundesbank, reported in Edwards and Fischer (1994).

The main point to be made here is the importance of non-financial corporations as shareholders. Companies hold shares in each other, partly in the form of cross-shareholdings and partly in the form of strategic stakes. Although banks have a relatively high level of importance, holding about 8% of the total equity, it is boosted by the fact that most individual shares are lodged with banks. This permits the banks, with the shareholder's agreement, to act as proxy for the shareholder, so strengthening its position. This is investigated further in chapter 9.

Individual share ownership

Information on share-ownership by individuals has been collected by ProShare, the UK shareholder lobby organisation. Table 8.4 provides comparative information for a number of European countries in 1991.

Table 8.4: Individual share ownership in different countries (1991)

Country	% held
Belgium	10
Finland	24
France	13
Germany	6
Great Britain	21
Sweden	26

Source: ProShare (1993).

These figures do not match exactly the earlier specific country ones, which may partly be because of timing differences and partly sampling procedures. Most importantly, this table reinforces the split between Anglo-Saxon-style economies and Continental European ones.

Pension-fund ownership

As shown in above, institutional shareholders are important in both the UK and Germany. Detailed information is not available on other European countries, but it is possible to infer the general level of importance from a consideration of other data. Table 8.5 provides information on the size of pension fund assets and their importance as a form of saving for the personal sector.

Table 8.5: Pension fund assets as a percentage of personal-sector assets (1988)

Country	Stock of assets ($ billion)	Personal-sector assets (%)
Denmark	13.1	–
France	27.7	3
Germany	41.1	2.4
Netherlands	177.4	29.6
Sweden	51.2	–
UK	475.9	27.2

Source: Davis.

This information places the overall assets of the pension funds in context but does not provide information on the split of these funds between different forms of assets. Table 8.6 provides this information, both as an average from 1970–90 and in the actual 1990 figure. Information is available, not only in terms of the importance of equities in the total holdings, but also for loans. This therefore provides an interesting comparator and a guide to the cost of these funds for corporations.

Table 8.6: Equities and loans as a percentage of assets

	Equities (as % of assets)		Loans (as % of assets)	
Country	**1990**	**Average**	**1990**	**Average**
Denmark	7.0	3.2	1.0	1.6
Germany	18.0	9.6	36.0	34.6
Netherlands	20.0	11.6	39.0	50.4
Sweden	1.0	0.2	10.0	20.8
UK	63.0	55.2	0.0	0.2

Source: Davis.

Table 8.6 shows that the UK's pension funds place a much greater proportion of their investments in equities than the other countries' funds. On the other hand, hardly any of their funds are ever lent while, in Germany and The Netherlands, this is an important use of funds. Whether the funds are invested in the UK because the stock market is relatively large in the UK, or the institutions have created such a large stock market by wanting to invest in this way, is unclear. What is clear is that the views and wishes of pension funds are likely to be given greater weight in the UK than in Continental European countries.

Relevance of the investor composition

The information on the importance of various shareholder categories has a bearing on the overall cost of capital to a company. There are two ways in which this shareholder pressure can be seen. Either through the dividend pay-out requirements or through the market for corporate control.

Dividend policy

One of the most important practical constraints on the cost of capital for a company is its dividend policy. Although economic theory suggests that dividends are nothing but a residual payment made by a company, once all profitable investment opportunities have been undertaken, reality shows that dividends are an important signalling tool. Investors are informed of the future prospects for a company through the payment of dividends. If they are increasing, the company is viewed positively by the markets.

Knowing the shareholder base is important in terms of understanding the way in which corporate dividend policy is established. In the UK, owing to the importance of tax-exempt financial institutions, especially pension funds, companies pay high levels of dividends. This maximises the income received by the shareholders but places a constraint on the operations of the company. Capital gains, either through retained earnings or scrip dividend issues, are less favoured, because of their relative tax disadvantage for financial institutions. This has been the subject of recent debate highlighted by the Trade and Industry Committee proceedings on the competitiveness of UK manufacturing industry (Trade and Industry Committee, 1994).

The UK's experience shows clearly that it is not only the shareholder base that is important, but also the way it interacts with the tax system. Taxation is considered in more detail in chapter 6. Comparative information on dividend payments is provided in Figures 2 and 3. The first is taken from the Confederation of British Industry's evidence to the Trade and Industry Committee and covers the whole economy, while the second concentrates on quoted companies in the UK and Germany.

Figures 2 and 3 show that, in the UK, companies pay out a higher proportion of profits to shareholders than in other countries. Two possible explanations can be put forward. First, UK companies are less profitable than their European counterparts—an argument which appears to carry little weight empirically. Second, dividends play a greater role in the UK.

Figure 2: Dividend payments as a percentage of net earnings of non-financial corporations (1982–93)

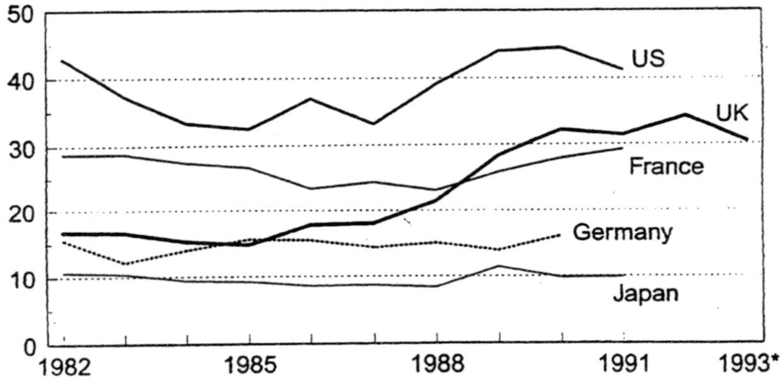

Note: The UK 1993 figure is for the first three quarters of 1993.
Source: Trade and Industry Committee (1994).

The takeover market

Another important way in which the shareholder profile affects corporate policy is through the effect it has on the market for corporate control. Anglo-Saxon markets place great emphasis on the activity of the takeover market as a correcting factor for managerial failure, while Continental European markets place much greater emphasis on other forms of control. These alternative approaches are discussed in detail later in this chapter. The difference between them is manifested in two ways.

First, the shareholder profile of Anglo-Saxon economies is biased towards individual shareholders—holding shares either directly or indirectly through financial institutions, such as pension funds—rather than corporate shareholders, as is the case

Figure 3: Dividend pay-out ratios (1982–88)

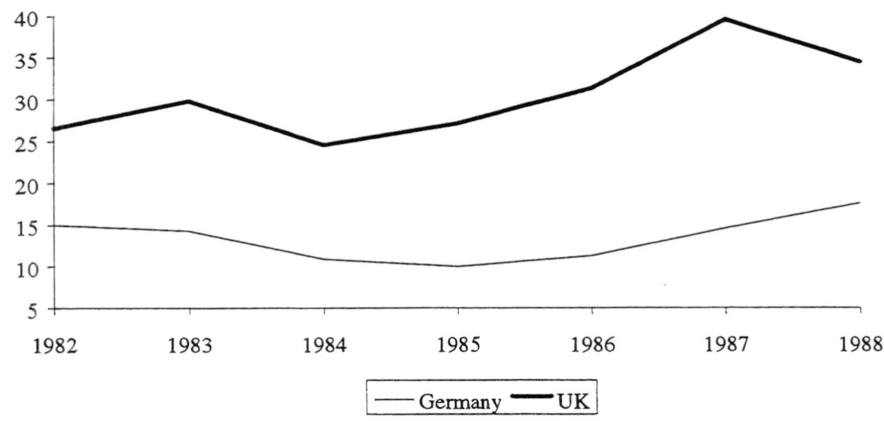

Source: Mayer and Alexander (1990).

in Continental Europe. Institutionalised forms of corporate shareholding, such as cross-shareholdings, are much more established on the Continent.

Second, the reliance on the equity markets for the implementation of corporate control leads to even greater significance being placed on the role of dividends. One possible explanation for the rapid rise in the dividend–pay-out ratio in the UK during the mid- to late 1980s was the influence of a merger wave. Paying ever-increasing dividends is an important way of keeping shareholders content with the incumbent management. This is not perceived to be a constraint on Continental European companies. In the UK, cutting, suspending or even holding stable a dividend payment is perceived to be a major sign of weakness, against which the market will react. In extreme cases it can even lead to a hostile takeover bid being launched. It is much more common for Continental European companies to be able to cut their dividends, especially if investment is to be undertaken with the funds, or some form of restructuring is to occur. One reason for this may be that, since banks play two roles, as major shareholders and as lenders to a company, they can adopt a different policy to that possible in an Anglo-Saxon economy, where shareholders and banks have divergent interests.

Linked to the two points above is the fact that the role attributed to the stock market in the UK, that of the primary corporate control mechanism, means that management decisions are effectively assessed. If a poor decision is made, either the company will become a target for a hostile bidder or the shareholders of the company will call for changes. A recent example of shareholder action in this way was linked to the Enterprise Oil bid for Lasmo. As the bid failed, shareholders called for changes to the management structure of the company, primarily the splitting of the job of Chief Executive and Chairman. The question of the almost 'supervisory' role of the stock market is returned to in chapter 9.

Problems of exit

One possible consequence of the difference between the Anglo-Saxon and Continental European investor bases is the problem of exit. Where an investor, whether it is the state or a private individual or company, holds a substantial stake in a company, they have less ability to walk away from their investment. A primary reason for the problem of being a 'locked-in' investor is the fact that selling a large shareholding could only be done at a substantial discount to the prevailing market price. Providing new finance for a company in difficulty—effectively what the state is doing through an aid programme—may prove to be a cheaper alternative to liquidating the investment. This implies that a straightforward cost-of-capital calculation for a company in financial difficulty may suggest a rate that is above the true rate that investors are willing to lend at. This possibility is investigated further in the following two sections.

Implications for the cost of capital

What are the implications of these shareholder differences for the cost of capital? In the UK the decision to raise quoted equity finance carries with it far greater significance than simply having to meet a specific cost of equity finance. Whether there is actual short-termism or whether it is just a perception of managers, the flotation of equity on the London Stock Exchange affects corporate policy. Dividend payments have to be met to ensure shareholder approval, thereby limiting the threat of takeover. This effectively implies a higher cost of capital than that which may be observed.

It is also important to note that, as the net flow of funds from equity is negative, the Stock Exchange does not provide 'real' investment funds at an aggregate level. Equity is raised to purchase other equity, ie, to acquire control of other companies. This means that the weight placed on the different forms of finance must be considered carefully.

In Continental Europe, even though companies may appear to have a relatively high cost of equity finance, according to the Coopers & Lybrand report, the greater flexibility offered by the investor profiles and the alternative forms of corporate control mean that, in practice, the cost of equity finance could be lower for an individual company. The way the shareholders react to a company in distress is very different, new funds may be provided with the knowledge of no, or low, dividends for a long period while restructuring takes place. This is obviously of relevance to state aid, as the aim is to assess how the private financial institutions would react to such a request for finance. So, it would appear that, if the funds are directly related to a restructuring, rather than for normal investment purposes, a lower cost of capital could be appropriate. However, quantifying this lower level of the cost of capital is difficult. This means that the calculated bench-mark should be seen more as a guide than a hard and fast figure.

Some of the alternative attitudes of Continental European providers of finance are considered in the next part of this chapter.

The relationship between banks and companies

As mentioned earlier in this chapter, banks in Germany are perceived to act very differently to those in the UK, owing to the different relationship that exists. Edwards and Fischer investigate this perceived difference in detail in their recent book and present a comprehensive survey of the available information (Edwards and Fischer, 1994). There is also some evidence in relation to France that will be drawn on at the end of this section. If different styles of relationship exist it could have an impact on the cost of capital estimated by the preferred approach.

There are five stylised facts that are put forward to explain why Germany's bank-based system is 'better' than a market system like that of the UK.

- German banks provide long-term finance to companies, while UK companies receive only short- and medium-term.

- Bank representation on the supervisory board of a company ensures that the usual principal–agent problems do not occur and the bank and company therefore work in harmony.

- There is less competition to provide loans as house banks exist. These help encourage the longer-term relationship.

- Banks are willing to help restructure companies and act in a longer-term sense than UK companies (see below).

- Loans to companies in other countries are assessed differently to those in the UK. Different collateral requirements exist between countries (see chapter 9).

Previous research has tended to accept these points while Edwards and Fischer's results have tended to question them. The first three statements are considered below.

Longer maturity of lending

The suggestion that German banks lend longer maturity loans to companies than those provided to UK companies has some superficial backing. Consider the evidence in Table 8.7.

Although there are problems in interpreting the data—for Germany the information relates to the original maturity of the loan, while, for the UK, it relates to the remaining maturity, and the definition of the banking sector is very different in the two countries—there does appear to be some difference between the countries. However, does this matter? As German loans are callable, the bank is not locked into a long-term loan and although a 15-year loan may be agreed at the outset, does this have a different impact from three five-year loans?

Also, the way the interest rate is set on a loan is important. Locking in a long-term loan at a low interest rate would obviously be beneficial. Yet, most medium-sized and larger companies can achieve the same effect through derivative instruments, such as swaps or forwards. This argument does not, therefore, appear to attract that much credence.

Table 8.7: Maturity of lending in Germany and the UK (%)

Original maturity of bank lending (excluding home loans) to domestic non-bank enterprises and self-employed persons in Germany:

	Short-term (< 1 year)	Medium-term (1–4 years)	Long-term (> 4 years)
1970	42.5	12.2	45.3
1980	39.5	9.3	51.2
1989	34.8	8.1	57.1

Residual maturity of lending to industry in the UK:

	Short-term (< 1 year)	Medium-term (1–4 years)	Long-term (> 4 years)
Clearing bank lending			
1980	67.0	20.0	13.0
1987	63.1	19.2	17.7
Total lending to industry			
1980	42.0	12.0	46.0
1987	50.8	15.5	33.7

Source: Monthly Report of the Deutsche Bundesbank; Vittas and Brown (1982) and Dicks (1989), reported in Edwards and Fischer (1994).

The importance of house banks

It is often assumed in the UK that a German company has one principal bank—often referred to as its house bank. The fact that there is this close relationship means that companies are treated differently from those in the UK, where there may be several competing banks. Although UK companies may have access to cheaper finance, owing to competition, the German house bank will stand by a company through both good and bad times. How true is this?

Table 8.8 provides information on the number of bank connections for German companies in the late 1970s, the most recent available information. It shows the percentage of companies in each size category that has a specific number of bank connections.

Table 8.8 appears to scotch the idea of there being house banks, although for a small percentage of one size category, there may be some justification for it. Overall, it would appear that German companies operate in the same way as UK companies; a group of banks is available with which the company has some level of connection and among which it can pick and choose.

Table 8.8: Number of bank connections

Company turnover (DM)	1	2–5	5–10	>10
Less than 25m	–	75.0	25.0	–
26–100m	7.7	38.5	38.5	15.3
101m–500m	–	40.4	36.2	23.4
Over 500	–	11.3	21.8	66.9

Source: Braun (1981), reported in Edwards and Fischer (1994).

Bank representation on the supervisory board

The final preconception to be considered in this sub-section is that of bank representation on the supervisory board of a company. Before considering the evidence, it is worth considering the role of the supervisory board.

German companies have two levels of board, the management or executive board and the supervisory board. The first of these is responsible for the day-to-day running of the company while the second, the supervisory board, is responsible for overseeing the management board and determining longer-term policy. Supervisory boards are composed of representatives of a company's stakeholders, eg shareholders and workers—through their unions—and, possibly, suppliers and distributors with whom the company has a close working relationship. Often these boards meet only twice a year and may therefore have little impact on immediate policy. However, management accounts are delivered to these boards, or specific members of the board, and so information is available to them.

There is a substantial body of evidence from previous surveys reported in Edwards and Fischer (1994) on bank representation on these boards. Two of the tables are reproduced below as Tables 8.9 and 8.10. Table 8.9 shows the importance of the banks quite clearly, especially Deutsche Bank, and this is reinforced by Table 8.10.

Again, this highlights the difference between the UK and Germany as the two largest shareholders, non-financial and financial corporations, provide over 50% of the total chairmen for companies in this size group. Few UK shareholders are of sufficient size, in terms of shareholding, to have the influence to select the chairman.

It is only in this third area, therefore, that the common myths seem to be vindicated and, even here, the usefulness of the position is not certain. Yet, these differences have traditionally been held to exist and to explain why German industry has proved more successful than that of the UK.

Two possible explanations for this problem can be put forward. First, the conclusions Edwards and Fischer draw from their research have contrasted with the findings of previous researchers. The balance of opinion may have swung too far against the impact of the bank–company relationship. Second, other recent research has highlighted the difference between the industrial mix of the two countries. In the UK R&D-intensive companies, especially those based on pharmaceuticals and electronics, have access to the 'venture' capital of the stock market while traditional industries, still the mainstay of German manufacturing, have access to the long-term bank

Table 8.9: Bank representation on supervisory boards of the largest 100 Aktiengesellschaften, by bank and type of seat (1974)

	Chairman	Deputy chairman	Simple membership	Total
Big banks	**21**	**19**	**62**	**102**
of which:				
Deutsche Bank	18	11	26	55
Dresdner Bank	2	6	18	26
Commerzbank	1	2	18	21
All other banks	**10**	**16**	**51**	**77**
of which:				
Regional and other commercial banks, and private bankers	8	15	34	57
Savings bank sector	1	1	5	7
Credit cooperative sector	1	–	2	3
Total	**31**	**35**	**113**	**179**

Source: Monopolkommission (1978), reported in Edwards and Fischer (1994).

Table 8.10: Type of shareholder representative acting as the chairman of the supervisory board of Aktiengesellschaften with more than 2,000 employees (1979)

Type of shareholder representative	% of total chairmen
Domestic non-banks	37.4
Domestic banks	19.2
Foreign companies	7.5
Government	9.7
Private shareholders	8.2
Former top executives	7.1
Consultants	11.0

Source: Gerum *et al.* (1988), reported in Edwards and Fischer (1994).

lending that is necessary. So, Edwards and Fischer's conclusions could be correct, as the difference in the financial systems is driven by the nature of the industrial companies rather than an inherent difference in practice.

Banks and financial distress

The fourth common perception, or misconception, is that banks in Continental Europe take a very different attitude to that adopted by UK banks when a company faces financial distress. Numerous cases are quoted where the UK attitude has conflicted with that of other European countries. Two such examples still fresh in the City's mind are Lancer Boss and Leyland DAF. High-profile support schemes occur occasionally. For example, when problems were found with International Signal, the US subsidiary of Ferranti, the banks supported the company. Also, the continuing support of Eurotunnel through its many problems is an example of banks taking a longer view—or, cynically, not being able to liquidate their collateral and so being forced to stay in, a similar concept to that of locked-in substantial-stake shareholders developed earlier. However, in the few cases of intervention that are quoted in the UK the Bank of England has often been behind the scenes persuading banks to be proactive.

It is claimed that German banks are much more willing to support a company through these sorts of trauma. Edwards and Fischer investigated two themes in this area. First, how do banks react to cases of financial distress? Second, owing to the closer relationship between banks and companies, are they better placed to detect potential problems and so solve them before a critical problem actually arises?

Result of financial distress

Table 8.11 details the results of a survey undertaken by Hesselmann and Stefan of 56 receivers and their actions during the period 1984–88.

Table 8.11: Continuation and liquidation of bankrupt companies, Germany, 1984–88

	Number	%
Total bankruptcy cases	2,106	100.0
Immediate liquidation	1,609	76.4
Attempt at rescue by debtor	81	3.8
of which: successful	55	2.6
Attempt at negotiated rescue	416	19.8
of which: successful	311	14.8

Source: Hesselmann and Stefan, reported in Edwards and Fischer (1994).

Table 8.11 illustrates quite plainly that, in the majority of cases, there was no attempt to rescue the bankrupt company. One possible explanation is the legal system in Germany for dealing with bankruptcy. Those companies that are saved appear to be saved outside the legal system rather than through it. Table 8.12 details the actions taken by a group of banks after financial distress has been detected. Again, this information is taken from a survey quoted in Edwards and Fischer and the results are based on a hypothetical company going into distress.

Table 8.12: Measures taken by German banks after financial distress has been detected

Measure	Number of banks taking measure
Cancellation and calling-in of loans	213
Advice to and influence on management	181
Obtaining additional collateral	141
Threat of opening bankruptcy proceedings	14
Securing collateral	10
Disclosure of assignments of assets	6
Forming a pool	3
Foreclosure proceedings	2
Total number of responses	570
Total number of banks responding	282

Source: Drukarcyk *et al.* (1985), reported in Edwards and Fischer (1994).

Again, this seems to suggest that German banks do not act very differently from UK banks; for the majority of them, their first consideration is the calling-in of the loan and the protection of their capital. Of course, as this was a hypothetical case the results may be misleading. As discussed earlier, unless a bank can easily call in its loans at little loss, the lack of exit may force a different, more supportive, response than the bank would theoretically like to follow.

Better bank monitoring

Although the banks do not appear particularly successful at saving companies, or reacting in any way differently from how a UK bank would behave once a loan has become problematic, does their privileged position provide them with a better ability to monitor companies and so implement a reorganisation before a company actually reaches its crisis point? Table 8.13 contains evidence from a survey of banks on their perceived ability to detect problem loans before a loss is incurred.

Table 8.13: German banks' ability to detect problem loans in time to avoid any losses

% of problem loans detected in time to avoid any losses	No. of banks responding	% of banks responding
>75–100	13	5.1
>50–75	77	30.0
>25–50	85	33.1
>0–25	71	27.6
0	11	4.3
Total	**257**	**100.0**

Source: Drukarcyk *et al.* (1985), reported in Edwards and Fischer (1994).

Apart from a small group of banks, the majority do not seem to be better informed than those in other countries. It would appear, therefore, that the privileged position they have does not make them better monitors of companies. This suggests that funds being provided by the state to financially distressed companies ought to be assessed in the same way as funds being provided for normal financing. However, the evidence provided here is only for Germany and is, in itself, not comprehensive.

Similar sentiment concerning the French system is often expressed. In France the links between banks and industrial companies exist in two ways, either through the complicated web of cross-shareholdings or through the conglomerates based around banks—eg, Groupe Indosuez based around Banque Indosuez, or the Paribas groupings. This is an area that has attracted less attention than the German bank–company relationship but could be expected to provide a similar impact on the cost of capital.

Implications for the bench-mark

It is important to realise the impact that institutional differences can have on the actual cost of capital. Once a bench-mark figure has been established, using the preferred methodology set out in chapters 3, 4, 6 and 7, it is necessary to consider why those figures need to be revised. Flexibility in relation to the cost of equity in Continental European countries, owing to the different shareholder base, could mean that what appears to be a high cost of capital, is actually lower. These types of consideration cannot be quantified easily and should therefore be seen as questions that have to be addressed, if a state aid evaluated under the MEIP yields a marginal pass or fail. The range of acceptable results should be altered according to the way that country's financial institutions operate.

Starting from the observation that dividend pay-out ratios are relatively high in the UK there appear to be several possible ways in which institutional differences can have an impact on the cost of capital. Relationships between banks and industrial companies appear to be very important in Continental Europe. Even though recent work by Edwards and Fischer has cast doubt on the significance of the impact of the relationship as it was traditionally perceived, it is impossible to get away from the initial observation concerning dividends. Clearly a different relationship between investors and companies exists, it just may not be explicable through the standard set of statements made concerning the role of banks.

There are also questions relating to the way in which lenders react to corporate financial distress. State aid can be considered as a form of support for companies in financial distress. If private lending organisations take a different attitude to lending to distressed companies—possibly owing to the problem of investors being 'locked in' to the relationship with no clear exit route that protects the value of the investment—rather than to other companies, the state aid should also be assessed at that different rate. Again, this does not invalidate the preferred methodology, it simply uses it as a base to which certain adjustments have to be made.

9. INVESTMENT-APPRAISAL TECHNIQUES

A final area where there may be differences between countries is that of investment appraisal. Even if a bench-mark figure is found using the preferred approach, if it differs substantially from the usual investment-appraisal approach undertaken in an economy, the bench-mark may need modification. There are three main groups whose attitudes to investment need to be assessed. They are:

- the companies undertaking the investment;
- banks and other lending institutions;
- brokers, since their attitudes determine those of equity investors.

Again, this is an area where only a little information for a limited number of countries is available. The available information employed here is drawn from:

- Edwards and Fischer (1994), who surveyed bank-lending practice in Germany and reported their findings;
- the Coopers & Lybrand study which considered the attitudes of 17 companies;
- brokers' reports on UK companies;
- evidence reported to the Trade and Industry Select Committee;
- anecdotal evidence from UK companies collected in earlier academic studies.

The three groups are considered in turn.

Company investment-decision behaviour

Although academic support for the CAPM and the WACC may be strong, few apart from the largest companies appear to follow the principle. Other methodologies appear to dominate. The two that are most commonly referred to are internal rates of return (IRR) or pay-back periods. Evidence on IRRs for various countries is presented in Figure 4.

The IRR effectively applies the WACC methodology, as it involves comparing the actual discount factor required to leave a project yielding a zero return, ie a net present value of zero, with a hurdle rate of return. This hurdle rate of return ought to be calculated using the methodology outlined in this book.

In Figure 4 it appears that the hurdle rate of return used by companies is quite different across countries. In the UK, over the period 1977–88, there are very few years in which the required rate of return is below 20%—presumably on a nominal

Figure 4: Required nominal internal rates of return (1977–88)

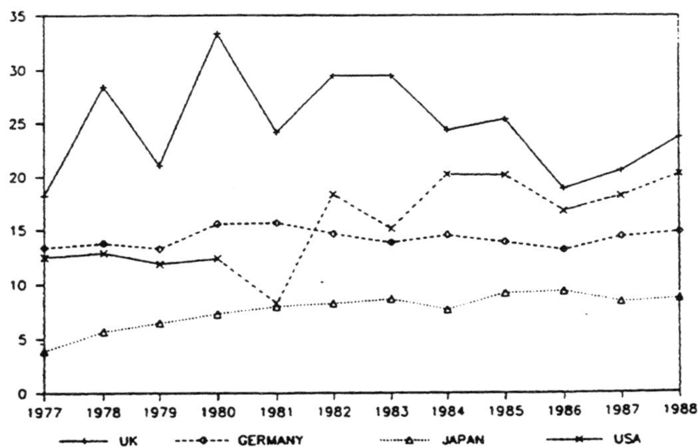

Source: Trade and Industry Committee (1994).

basis. In Germany, however, where the cost of capital would appear to be higher than in the UK, a much lower IRR is employed—it hardly ever goes above 15%. Although in the early part of the period it could be argued that high and unpredictable inflation rates could cause this great a difference, the fact that it persists during the mid-1980s when the UK economy was much more stable, suggests that another, more fundamental, reason should be sought. An argument could be constructed around the perceived short-termism of the stock market in London. Anecdotal evidence would suggest that companies seek to achieve a higher rate of return over as short a time period as possible to ensure that investors' expectations are satisfied.

The Coopers & Lybrand study's approach to this question was different. It took 17 companies from various member countries—five from the UK, three from each of Italy and The Netherlands, and two from each of Portugal, France and Germany—as the source of case-study material on how the cost of capital was employed when they decided whether to undertake investments.

A number of key results were obtained from interviewing personnel at these companies:

- the majority of them did not consider the cost of capital directly, although some parts of it proved important. These were the level of gearing, the price and availability of equity capital for smaller companies and the level of short-term interest rates;

- tax was considered an important factor, especially in relation to cash flow rather than the actual cost of capital.

Again, other UK anecdotal evidence would support the findings of these interviews. Companies tend either to apply simple investment rules, such as pay-back, or to consider internal hurdle rates of return, where the hurdle may be set higher than an equivalent cost of capital rate.

This evidence appears to suggest that some of the claims concerning 'short-termism' in the UK are correct, in as much as rates of return in excess of the cost of capital are expected. Whether this exists because of the attitudes of investors, discussed later, or because managers expect the market to expect high rates of return is not clear. It does, however, tie in with the role of the stock market as a supervisor of corporate decisions that was discussed previously. Setting high hurdle rates of return may be the managers' way of proving that they are capable and prudent managers.

A survey carried out by the Confederation of British Industry (CBI) in May 1994—published in July 1994—attempted to establish how companies actually assess their investment programmes. Several questions were investigated, including the mix of judgemental and quantitative methods, definition of the rate of return, factors influencing the rate of return and the impact of expected inflation. Table 9.1 contains the salient points of the survey.

Table 9.1: Results of the CBI survey

Question	%
Undertake quantitative assessment	90
Of those companies answering yes, the methodology employed was:	
an accounting rate	13
a discounted cash-flow rate	53
simple payback	75
return on capital	49
return on equity	12
other	3
The required rate of return is calculated on a:	
pre-tax basis	56
post-tax basis	41
The required rate of return is based on:	
real figures	35
nominal figures	63
For those that use real figures, the mean is	16.4
For those that use nominal, the mean is	16.8
Those companies using nominal data expect the average annual inflation rate to be	4.9
Sensitivity analysis is employed	48

Source: CBI, 1994.

The table shows quite clearly that the majority of companies employ several quantitative measures when assessing new investment projects. The distinctions drawn between these different approaches are somewhat arbitrary, since underlying any payback approach is an implicit rate of return. There are several additional questions, the results of which are not presented here, that suggest something akin to the CAPM is employed in establishing the rate of return, although no formal question referring to this was asked.

Another indication of the importance of CAPM-style calculations was provided by questions on the establishment of the hurdle rate. Ignoring inflation, the most important factor was the riskiness of the project. However, rather than quantitatively establishing the relative riskiness, the majority of companies considered subjective measures.

This survey produced many useful pieces of information relating to the way in which industry assesses its investment in the UK. Unfortunately there were many more questions that were not investigated in this survey.

Bank-lending criteria

A number of factors determine how banks decide whether to provide finance for a company. Table 9.2 presents information on the criteria applied by German banks when determining whether to provide short- or medium-term finance.

Table 9.2: Criteria considered in German lending decisions

Factor	Weighted relative frequency
Good profitability and liquidity	34.1
Quality of management	24.2
First-rank mortgages as collateral	15.3
Nature of project financed by loan	10.8
Debt ratio	7.8
Mobile assets as collateral	6.6
Other	1.1
Negative pledge	0.1

Source: Drukarcyk *et al.* (1985), reported in Edwards and Fischer (1994).

It would appear that, rather than consider the actual rate of return a project is expected to make, or even its risk profile, banks are happy to lend if the management is good or if collateral is available. Profitability and liquidity is important, but for the company rather than for a specific project. The question of collateral is investigated further in Table 9.3.

Table 9.3: The significance of various types of collateral for short- and medium-term bank loans

Type	Average share in total volume of loans	Average share by number of loans
Real estate (mortgage, etc)	31.2	26.9
Mobile assets	34.4	48.8
Other forms of collateral	4.0	3.8
Total collateralised loans	69.9	79.5
Unsecured loans	30.4	20.5

Source: Drukarcyk *et al.* (1985), reported in Edwards and Fischer (1994).

Of all German bank loans, 70% are collateralised, hence the level of interest in the returns on a project is low, as the banks have insured themselves through the provision of collateral.

Before any conclusions can be drawn from this in relation to state aid, there has to be a consideration of the relevance of these studies to large companies. There is, however, anecdotal evidence from the UK that suggests that, even for the largest companies, banks prefer to protect themselves through collateral rather than an evaluation of the individual project. It would appear that, in the case of Lancer Boss, one of the reasons why the receivers were called in was to protect the collateral of the banks and ensure that any solution did not unduly harm the assets set aside to provide collateral.

It should, of course, be noted that the question about collateralisation is in some ways redundant when discussing state aid. If the government demands collateral from the public enterprise in return for aid all that the government is achieving is the possible transfer of assets that it already indirectly owns, as the company is a public enterprise, to its direct ownership. So, although collateralisation is an important question when considering bank lending practice it is actually of little use when examining the state-aid question.

Equity analysts' expectations

In the UK financial institutions are expected to be the most informed investor group. Equity analysts spend a long time researching companies and determining whether an investment in the company is worthwhile. Important to this decision is the cost of equity finance, specifically, and the cost of capital, in general.

Reports of brokers and analysts have traditionally been viewed as documents aimed at encouraging the buying and selling of equity. However, some of the larger financial institutions also use them to disseminate information relating to the research undertaken by a company's employees. Four quite significant 1992 reports, by County Natwest and UBS Phillips & Drew, are listed in the references. These consider what the true cost of equity finance ought to be and come down very heavily in favour of the new *ex ante* approaches to establishing the value. It would appear, therefore, that equity investors take these considerations seriously and follow through the methodologies that this book has outlined.

Implications for the bench-mark

What do these comments on the decision-making process used for investments have to do with the cost of capital? First, some of the evidence suggests that the approach set out is the correct one. Knowing the cost of capital for a company allows informed investors to determine whether the investment should go ahead. What may be in doubt, if evidence from the UK is believed, is whether the way in which the hurdle rate of return is established necessarily follows the preferred methodology set out in this book.

Second, the actual cost may not be as important as believed. Provided sufficient collateral is available, German banks appear willing to lend to companies. However, collateralisation is not possible for direct state aid, as explained earlier, although if the government were providing guarantees for external finance, collateralisation is another way in which the cost of that finance could be lowered. The overall relevance of this question for the MEIP is unlikely to be significant.

10. CONCLUSIONS AND THE IMPLICATIONS FOR DIFFERENCES IN BENCH-MARKS FOR STATE-AID ANALYSES ACROSS COUNTRIES

The cost of capital is a robust and powerful tool in finance. Applying it to the question of state aid provides an easily understood bench-mark against which any proposed government injection of funds can be measured. However, there are some problems with its applications and a grey area is likely to exist, therefore, in which some projects that fail the bench-mark test will then be deemed acceptable. Each of these points is summarised below.

Preferred methodology

Chapters 3 to 7 developed the preferred methodology for calculating the cost of capital. The two principal components, the cost of debt and the cost of equity, both have traditional and new approaches. In most cases, it is the new approach that is preferred.

The cost of debt

The cost of debt should be measured as a premium over the risk-free rate. In order of preference, the premium should be calculated as:

- the difference between the observed redemption yields of the company and a government comparator bond. These should be measured in the Euro-markets;
- an estimated difference arising from an econometric model incorporating Euro-market data of other companies' observed debt premia;
- the difference between the observed redemption yields of the company and a government comparator bond in the domestic debt markets;
- an estimated difference arising from an econometric model incorporating domestic market data of other companies' observed debt premia;
- the observed premium paid over bank base rates on term loans.

The cost of equity
The cost of equity should be calculated through the CAPM. Three elements need to be estimated:

- *risk-free rate*, which should be the redemption yield on an index-linked bond or the redemption yield on a nominal bond, minus the expected inflation rate over a similar period;

- *ERP*, for which an *ex ante* estimate should be found. If that is not possible, a mixed version or an historical version are the only real alternatives;

- *risk of the company*, measured through its beta estimate. Where a company is quoted, the calculation should be based on five years' worth of data with all three options—daily, weekly and monthly—considered. Where the company is not quoted, information should be sought from comparable companies, preferably within the same country but, if necessary, from another country. If this latter approach has to be undertaken, it is important to find the closest possible comparator.

Taxation
The impact of tax should be assessed. It is standard to ignore the impact of depreciation and capital allowances. In the case of airlines, however, this should also be considered because of their level of profitability and their reliance on leasing finance. Standard taxation factors are available, any changes in the tax system need to be incorporated.

Weighted average cost of capital
The weight that should be applied to each type of finance can be measured in two ways. It is normal to use the gearing figure, an average measure of the existing capital structure. However, in terms of data availability and the applicability of the result, the preferred approach would be to use the net flow-of-funds estimate of the use of each type of finance. These values should, however, be checked against each other. Flow-of-funds information provides an indication of the financing proportions of the marginal projects being undertaken by companies rather than the historical average capital structure. When comparisons are being made between international companies it is very important to ensure that if gearing figures are employed the impact of inflation and any differences in book valuation techniques have been properly accounted for.

Restrictions on its application
Problems exist in terms of the application of the preferred methodology. Some of these are data problems and possible solutions have been suggested above. Others are more difficult to solve.

Institutional differences

Owing to institutional differences—the size of the stock market and the composition of the investor base—it is expected that companies act differently in different countries. This may have an impact on the cost of capital and should be assessed carefully. In particular, the willingness of investors in Continental European companies to accept dividend freezes, or even cuts, may make the actual cost of equity finance lower than it appears in those countries.

Investment criteria

If the criteria that investors use to determine whether they are going to invest in a company or project differ, it may also have an impact on the cost of capital. Primarily, it may be the case that Continental European banks take a longer-term view, owing to their greater interaction with companies than that of their Anglo-Saxon counterparts. Again, this could mean that any bench-mark figure found is actually higher than the true cost of capital.

Non-listed companies

Most airlines, for example, are not quoted on a stock exchange but are either private companies or state enterprises. This creates a problem in terms of the amount of available information to construct the preferred methodology. Although proxy values can often be found from comparable companies these are bound to introduce a degree of uncertainty to the values derived.

Recommendations

This book has attempted to undertake a systematic evaluation of the determinants of the cost of capital for state-aid assessments. It has considered a range of methodologies that are commonly employed in cost-of-capital studies. It has examined the different components of the cost of capital and evaluated the robustness of the results that emerge. The book has considered the applicability of the standard analyses to international comparisons of the cost of capital and discussed the extent to which international differences in financial markets affect these comparisons.

The conclusion of the study is that there are well-established methodologies for determining the costs of capital. There are significant questions raised by the implementation of these methodologies. In particular, there is much uncertainty about the appropriate level of risk premia in the CAPM. The traditional values that have been commonly employed in CAPM studies may have been too high on account of a failure to take adequate account of unanticipated inflation.

Other areas of the CAPM are less contentious, though there are still serious methodological questions concerned with the determination of riskless rates of return, beta coefficients and tax wedges. More seriously, the CAPM approach does not translate easily into international comparisons. There are marked differences in the size of stock markets across countries that call into question the relevance of stock-market estimates. International comparisons of risk premia and beta coefficients are fraught with difficulty. International comparisons of riskless returns and tax wedges are less problematic.

International comparisons of costs of capital must, therefore, be treated with considerable caution. However, there are more fundamental problems that arise. The structure of capital markets displays marked differences across countries. Patterns of ownership and control of companies vary appreciably. This bears crucially on the cost of capital that companies face. Large shareholders that are committed to their companies may take quite different views about returns that accrue in the future from dispersed shareholders. Relations between banks and industry differ across countries and affect the terms on which companies raise finance. These effects are very difficult to quantify, but they could be of considerable importance in the determination of international differences in costs of capital.

This further serves to emphasise the importance of exercising caution in the application of international comparisons. It does not imply that such comparisons should not be undertaken. Since bench-marks are required in state-aid investigations, there really is little alternative. However, the institutional differences across countries can be used to influence the debate. Close bank relations on the Continent may lower costs of capital when companies are in financial distress. Lower dividend pay-outs outside the UK may matter, despite theory suggesting that distinctions between dividends and capital gains are irrelevant from the point of shareholders.

A final complication with the preferred methodology is that as the question being addressed by the book, that of state aid, is normally provided to state-owned companies that are not listed, many of the components required for the calculation of the cost of capital are not available. In some ways these problems are exacerbated by the difficulty of making international comparisons, since another dimension is being introduced to the question, while in other ways—particularly in terms of the availability of quoted comparator companies—international studies can actually improve the availability of data.

It is suggested, therefore, that this book be used to provide an indication of the way in which costs of capital should be determined and that the problems of computing costs of capital for unlisted companies or in an international context should be borne in mind. The effects of potentially mis-specified proxy values and institutional differences across countries should then be incorporated into discussion in a more qualitative fashion. Also, the availability of other corroborating evidence should not be overlooked. Although CAPM is the preferred approach it is not the only one and in those cases where doubt about the constituents of CAPM exist, these other methodologies should be employed to provide additional evidence.

APPENDIX 1: THE RESULTS OF THE COOPERS & LYBRAND STUDY

Country	Real cost of equity	Real cost of debt	Debt–equity ratio	Real cost of capital (without tax)	Tax wedge	Real pre-tax cost of capital
Italy	15.1	8.6	0.75	12.0	4.3	16.3
Germany	16.1	9.3	1.00	12.6	4.9	17.5
France	22.1	12.4	1.44	16.2	1.6	17.7
Belgium	23.6	10.4	1.27	16.0	2.7	18.7
UK	16.0	7.7	0.20	14.3	5.7	19.9
Netherlands	20.6	8.9	0.64	15.8	4.6	20.4
Spain	27.9	7.0	0.75	18.4	6.8	25.2
Denmark	17.4	9.0	1.86	11.8	1.4	13.2
Luxemburg	17.8	9.6	1.27	13.1	3.5	16.6
Portugal	18.7	11.9	1.00	14.8	2.8	17.6
Greece	21.7	20.3	3.00	20.5	–1.9	18.6
Ireland	20.6	6.7	0.15	18.5	1.0	19.5

Note: All figures are percentages except the debt–equity ratio.

APPENDIX 2: BLANCHARD'S REAL RISK-FREE INTEREST RATES

Medium-term real interest rates % (1978–93)

Year	UK	Germany	France	Italy
1978	0.1	1.4	2.4	4.5
1979	4.5	2.4	–0.1	1.1
1980	4.1	3.3	3.2	1.9
1981	2.1	4.9	3.9	1.8
1982	5.3	5.7	3.3	7.4
1983	2.3	4.0	6.3	5.1
1984	3.3	3.9	5.1	3.8
1985	5.8	4.6	4.3	3.2
1986	6.7	3.7	4.2	6.5
1987	6.7	4.0	5.6	3.2
1988	4.7	3.5	6.9	3.7
1989	4.9	4.1	5.2	4.1
1990	7.2	5.3	6.8	6.8
1991	6.4	6.1	6.7	5.8
1992	6.0	4.9	4.9	3.2
1993	3.1	4.3	5.2	6.6

APPENDIX 3: JENKINSON'S *EX ANTE* ESTIMATES OF THE EQUITY RISK PREMIUM

Panel A

These estimates assume perfect foresight of *long-run* inflation and *long-run* rates of real dividend growth. Inflation forecasts are produced for year t by calculating the actual (geometric) average inflation rate from period t to t+20 (reflecting the 20-year average life of the bonds in the index). For the years from 1974 onwards, for which less than 20 years' future data is available, the average is computed over all the remaining years up to 1993. The dividend growth forecasts are produced by calculating the actual (geometric) average rate of real dividend growth forward for each year up to 1993. Thus, for more recent years, the averages will be computed over shorter time periods than the earlier years. All figures are percentages.

	1920–1993		1946–1993		1963–1993	
	A	U	A	U	A	U
Geometric averages						
Equity returns	6.68	0.82	6.62	0.03	7.29	–0.87
Gilt returns	1.38	0.88	1.28	–1.23	3.11	–1.19
Risk premium	5.29	–0.06	5.34	1.26	4.17	0.32
Arithmetic averages						
Equity returns	6.73	3.10	6.69	2.49	7.34	2.23
Gilt returns	1.47	1.70	1.41	–0.62	3.26	–0.56
Risk premium	5.26	1.39	5.29	3.11	4.08	2.79

Note: A = anticipated; U = unanticipated.

Panel B

These estimates assume that expected rate of real dividend growth and inflation expectations are formed by a weighted average of the previous five years' actual outturns with the weights declining exponentially.

	1920–1993		1946–1993		1963–1993	
	A	**U**	**A**	**U**	**A**	**U**
Geometric averages						
Equity returns	6.61	0.42	6.67	0.03	7.29	–0.87
Gilt returns	1.92	–0.31	1.44	–1.38	1.78	0.15
Risk premium	4.69	0.73	5.23	1.36	4.66	–0.17
Arithmetic averages						
Equity returns	6.75	2.41	6.79	2.40	6.52	3.04
Gilt returns	2.04	0.31	1.56	–0.78	1.96	0.73
Risk premium	4.72	2.10	5.23	3.18	4.56	2.31

APPENDIX 4: NUMERICAL EXAMPLE OF BETA DECOMPOSITION

The beta value for a state-owned airline is sought. The closest comparator is a company with three divisions, airlines, airport operation and freight, which has an observed group equity beta of 0.7. Table A4.1 provides information on the group and its divisions.

Table A4.1: The comparator company

Division	Net asset proportion	Gearing
Group	1.00	0.27
Airlines	0.50	0.30
Airport	0.40	0.20
Freight	0.10	0.40

Now, the proxies for the airport operation and freight divisions are given in Table A4.2.

Table A4.2: Proxy information

Proxy	Observed beta	Gearing	Asset beta
Airport	0.40	0.30	0.28
Freight	1.10	0.60	0.44

Employing this asset beta information, equity betas for the two divisions of the group can be established. For airports a value of 0.35 is found—0.28 divided by 0.8—while for freight a value of 0.73 is found.

Using this information, the airline equity beta value can be found:

$$0.7 = (\beta_A \times 0.5) + (0.35 \times 0.4) + (0.73 \times 0.1)$$
$$0.7 = 0.5\beta_A + 0.21$$
$$0.5\beta_A = 0.49$$
$$\beta_A = 0.98$$

This value, once adjusted to become an asset beta, could then be used as a proxy for the state-owned airline's beta value.

REFERENCES

Bank of England (1994), 'Inflation Report', May.

Barclays de Zoete Wedd (1994), *Equity Gilt Study 1919–1993*.

Blanchard, O. (1993), 'Movements in the Equity Premium', *Brookings Papers on Economic Activity*.

Blume, M. E. (1974), 'Unbiased Estimators of Long-run Expected Rates of Return', *Journal of the American Statistical Association*, **69**(347), 634–8.

Braun P. A. (1981), 'Das Firmenkundengeschäft der Banken im Wandel', University of Augsburg, unpublished Ph.D. thesis.

British Airways, (1992), *Report and Accounts 1991–92*.

CAA (1993), 'Airline Competition in the Single European Market', Civil Aviation Authority.

CBI (1994), 'Realistic Returns: How Do Manufacturers Assess New Investment?', Confederation of British Industry.

Consensus Forecasts (1994), May and August.

Cooper, I. (1993), 'Arithmetic versus Geometric Mean Risk Premia: Setting Discount Rates for Capital Budgeting', IFA Working Paper 174–93.

Coopers & Lybrand, 'Final Report for Study on International Differences in the Cost of Capital for the European Commission', unpublished.

Corbett, J., and Jenkinson, T. J. (1993), 'The Financing of Industry, 1970–89: An International Comparison', University of Oxford, mimeo.

County Natwest (1992*a*), 'The Equity Risk Premium Puzzle', *Equity Briefing*.

County Natwest (1992*b*), 'Solving the Risk Premium Puzzle', *Equity Briefing*.

Davis, E. P., 'The Structure, Regulation and Performance of Pension Funds in Nine Industrial Countries', paper for World Bank project, 'Income Security for Old Age', mimeo.

Dicks, M. J. (1989), 'A Cross-country Comparison of the Links between the Financial System and Industry', Bank of England, unpublished paper.

Drukarcyk, J. *et al.* (1985), *Mobiliarsicherheiten, Arten, Verbreitung, Wirksamkeit*, Köln, Bundesanzeiger.

Edwards, J. S. S., and Fischer, K. (1994), *Banks, Finance and Investment in Germany*, Cambridge, Cambridge University Press.

European Commission (1992), 'Report of the Committee of Independent Experts on Company Taxation'.

European Commission (1991/92), 'The Cost of Capital'.

Federal Reserve Bank of New York (1989), 'Explaining International Differences in the Cost of Capital'.

Gerum, E., Steinmann, H. and Fees, W. (1988), *Der mitbestimmte Aufsichtsrat—eine empirische Untersuchung*, Stuttgart, Poeschel Verlag.

Hesselmann, S. and Stefan, U. (1990), *Zerschlagung oder Sanierung von Unternehmen bei Insolvenz*, Stuttgart, Institut für Mittelstandsforschung Bonn.

Jenkinson, T. J. (1994), 'The Equity Risk Premium and the Cost of Capital Debate in the UK Regulated Utilities', University of Oxford, mimeo.

King, M., and Fullerton, D. (1984), *The Taxation of Income from Capital*, Chicago, Chicago University Press.

London Stock Exchange (1994*a*), *Fact Book 1994*.

London Stock Exchange (1994*b*) *Quality of Markets*, spring edition.

Mayer, C. P. (1990), 'Financial Systems, Corporate Finance, and Economic Development', in R. G. Hubbard (ed.), *Asymmetric Information, Corporate Finance, and Investment*, NBER.

Mayer C. P., and Alexander, I. (1990), 'Banks and Securities Markets: Corporate Financing in Germany and the United Kingdom', *Journal of The Japanese and International Economies*, **3**(4).

Monopolies and Mergers Commission (1993), *Gas and British Gas plc*, CM 2317, London, HMSO.

Monopolkommission (1978), *Hauptgutachten II: Fortschreitende Konzentration bei Grossunternehmen*, Baden-Baden, Nomos Verlag.

Moody's (1994), *Global Ratings Guide*, May.

OFGAS (1992), 'Estimating the Rate of Return for Gas Transportation', Office of Gas Supply.

OFWAT (1991), 'The Cost of Capital: A Consultation Paper', volumes 1–3, Office of Water Services.

ProShare (1993), 'Information on Share Ownership'.

Spackman, M. (1991), 'Discount Rates and Rates of Return in the Public Sector: Economic Issues', Government Economic Service Working Paper No. 113 and Treasury Working Paper No. 58.

Trade and Industry Committee (1994), *Competitiveness of UK Manufacturing Industry*, Second Report, London, HMSO.

UBS Phillips & Drew (1992*a*), 'Looking Beyond the Recession'.

UBS Phillips & Drew (1992*b*), 'A Brief History of Investment'.

Vittas, D., and Brown, R. (1982), 'Bank Lending and Industrial Investment: A Response to Recent Criticisms', Banking Information Service, unpublished paper.

WSA (1991), 'The Cost of Capital in the Water Industry', Water Services Association.